D0760854

SIEGES
THAT CHANGED
THE WORLD

ALAMO

CONSTANTINOPLE

DIEN BIEN PHU

MASADA

PETERSBURG

STALINGRAD

DIEN BIEN PHU

RICHARD WORTH

SERIES CONSULTING EDITOR
TIM McNEESE
YORK COLLEGE

CHELSEA HOUSE
P U B L I S H E R S
A Haights Cross Communications Company
Philadelphia

FRONTIS Map of Southeast Asia. On this map, Dien Bien Phu is in the
northwestern corner of North Vietnam.

CHELSEA HOUSE PUBLISHERS

VP, NEW PRODUCT DEVELOPMENT Sally Cheney
DIRECTOR OF PRODUCTION Kim Shinners
CREATIVE MANAGER Takeshi Takahashi
MANUFACTURING MANAGER Diann Grasse

STAFF FOR CONSTANTINOPLE

EXECUTIVE EDITOR Lee Marcott
PRODUCTION EDITOR Jaimie Winkler
PICTURE RESEARCHER Noelle Nardone
SERIES & COVER DESIGNER Keith Trego
LAYOUT 21st Century Publishing and Communications, Inc.

A Haights Cross Communications ◆ Company

http://www.chelseahouse.com

First Printing

1 3 5 7 9 8 6 4 2

Library of Congress Cataloging-in-Publication Data

Worth, Richard.
    Dien Bien Phu / Richard Worth.
       p. cm.—(Sieges that changed the world)
Includes index.
Summary: Describes the historical background, events, and aftermath of
the 1954 battle at Dien Bien Phu, which led to the end of the first
Indochina War.
    ISBN 0-7910-7228-2
    1. Diéen Biéen Ph(r)u (Vietnam), Battle of, 1954—Juvenile literature.
[1. Diéen Biéen Ph(r)u (Vietnam), Battle of, 1954. 2. Indochinese War,
1946–1954. 3. Vietnam—History—20th century.] I. Title. II. Series.
DS553.3.D5 W67 2002
959.704'142—dc21
                                                    2002012913

TABLE of CONTENTS

The son of a civil servant, Ho Chi Minh grew up to become Vietnam's strongest Communist leader. His charismatic personality won him followers and helped him lead his people in their fierce fight to end French rule.

1

Decision at Dien Bien Phu

In May 1953, a plane landed at the airport outside Hanoi, Vietnam, bringing the new French military commander to Indochina. His name was Henri Navarre. He was a thin, gray-haired veteran of the French army. General Navarre faced an enormous challenge in French Indochina, which included not only Vietnam but also the neighboring countries of Laos and Cambodia. For almost ten years, the French had been involved in a guerrilla war against the Communist Viet Minh. Now the French army seemed to be losing. The morale of the troops was low as they faced an enemy that seemed to be able to strike almost anywhere, then disappear quickly into the deep forests. Many soldiers seemed to believe that the Viet Minh could not be defeated.

Although the French controlled the major cities of Vietnam, such as Hanoi in the north and Saigon in the south, they could not stop the Viet Minh in the countryside. The Communists staged hit-and-run attacks in the Tonkin area, east of Hanoi; in central Vietnam, called Annam; as well as in the Mekong River Delta, around Saigon. Most recently, the Viet Minh had also been threatening nearby Laos.

Navarre looked at the situation carefully. His army included about 175,000 troops. More than half were needed to defend the French positions in the major cities. This left only about 75,000 soldiers free to attack the Viet Minh. After considering his options, he devised what became known as the Navarre Plan. It called for the French to stay on the defense. They would, however, launch attacks against Communist positions throughout Vietnam. They would try to keep the Viet Minh off balance, especially north of Hanoi, near Laos. To defend Laos, Navarre decided to occupy Dien Bien Phu, a village, in the northern highlands, near the Laotian border. This position had fallen into the hands of the Viet Minh a few months earlier. Navarre decided to push them out and use Dien Bien Phu as a base for attacking the Communists if they advanced into Laos. Navarre discussed his plans with his second-in-command, General Rene Cogny. He was a tall, heavy-set man whom Navarre had promoted. Once the plan was under way, Cogny was ordered to capture Dien Bien Phu. It fell to the French in the fall of 1953.

In the northern hills of Vietnam where they maintained their military bases, the Viet Minh watched the French operations. Meanwhile, Communist leader Ho Chi Minh and his closest associate, General Vo Nguyen Giap, were planning their own campaign. Ho Chi Minh was now over 60 years old, but he still kept up a rigorous schedule that included daily exercise and frequent meetings with Communist officials. He traveled throughout the northern highlands, inspiring the soldiers of the Viet Minh to keep up the struggle against the French.

At first, Ho and Giap had planned an operation that was similar to Navarre's. It called for guerrilla attacks throughout Vietnam to retain control of the countryside. Giap also hoped that the Viet Minh might be able to launch an assault on Hanoi. Ho feared that the Communists were not strong enough to win such a battle, though. He was supported by his strong ally Mao Zedong. Mao had established a Communist government in China in 1949, and he was supplying the Viet Minh with large quantities of military supplies. These included ammunition, food, and trucks to transport Viet Minh troops.

Ho and Giap stuck to their original plan until November 1953. At that time, the French recaptured Dien Bien Phu. Suddenly, the two Communist leaders saw an opportunity. If they could concentrate Viet Minh troops on the hills surrounding Dien Bien Phu, they might catch the French in a trap. Dien Bien Phu was near the Viet Minh home base and also close to the Chinese border. Therefore, the Viet Minh could easily supply a large army there. They could also continue to receive supplies from the Chinese Communists. Dien Bien Phu was 200 miles (322 kilometers) from Hanoi, which made it far more difficult for the French to supply.

If the Viet Minh surrounded Dien Bien Phu, Navarre might be tempted to rush in reinforcements to prevent the Viet Minh from winning a major victory. Such a loss would be a terrible blow to French honor in Indochina. On the other hand, Navarre could not afford to concentrate too many men there, because he had so much other territory to defend. This might give the Viet Minh an advantage, enable their army to outnumber the French, and help them win a great victory. If that occurred, it might force France into negotiations over Indochina. The

General Henri Navarre was commander-in-chief of the French forces at Dien Bien Phu. Some of the decisions he made may have given the Viet Minh forces an advantage during the fateful siege.

French had already indicated a willingness to negotiate because they were not winning the war—and because the war was not very popular with the French people. A loss at Dien Bien Phu might convince the French that the time had come to leave Vietnam.

Of course, there were risks. Ho and Giap recognized the problems. The Vietnam had never faced the French in a large battle. Usually, the fighting had been small conflicts. Giap was prepared to gamble that the Viet Minh were ready for a major confrontation with the French, however. His soldiers had been rigorously trained. They were intensely loyal to him. They were also Vietnamese people who wanted to drive the French out of their homeland. In addition, the Chinese had given their full support to Giap's plan.

In December 1953, Ho and Giap decided that the time had come to go ahead with their change in strategy. They ordered a major concentration of Viet Minh forces at Dien Bien Phu. A decision had been made that would change the course of history in Southeast Asia.

A Land
Called Vietnam

In the thirteenth century, Italian merchant Marco Polo traveled to China, where he had a lengthy stay at the court of Mongol Emperor Kublai Khan. The two men are seen here during Polo's visit. Kublai Khan controlled a vast territory that included what later became the nation of Vietnam.

Indochina is a long peninsula in Southeast Asia. The peninsula received the name Indochina because its culture had been influenced by both India and China. About 2,000 years ago, merchants from these two countries traded in Indochina. India had a profound impact on countries in the southern part of the peninsula, such as Thailand. The Chinese culture influenced countries in the north, such as Vietnam.

Between 500 B.C. and 300 B.C., people from Mongolia and China began to settle in northern Vietnam. The Mongolian settlers were called Viets. Their name gave the country its original name, Nam Viet. About 200 B.C., a Chinese general named Trieu Da conquered the northern part of the country. He wanted to be independent of China, and for a century, Vietnam remained that way. Around 100 B.C., however, Chinese armies invaded and took control of the area. They were much too powerful to be stopped.

The Chinese brought many improvements to Vietnam. In the north, the land around the Red River was a fertile rice-growing area. The Chinese improved the farmland in the Red River Delta. They introduced new farm implements, such as the metal plow. The Chinese also imported a large animal called the water buffalo to pull a farmer's plow. The use of water buffaloes helped farmers cultivate more land.

In addition to better farm methods, the Chinese also changed the culture of Vietnam. For example, they introduced Confucianism. Confucius was a Chinese philosopher who lived from about 551 to 479 B.C. He developed a system of ethical principles that were designed to guide every Chinese family. Confucius taught that the Chinese father was head of the family and deserved obedience. In turn, he was expected to run his family according to high moral principles. The same concept applied to the nation. The emperor deserved obedience, but only if he governed wisely and fairly. The writings of Confucius also guided the people who ran the bureaucracy. These officials, called mandarins, were expected to pass difficult examinations that showed their mastery of Confucius's philosophy.

The Chinese began to change the Vietnamese government so that its officials followed the teachings of Confucius. China also introduced the religious principles of Buddhism into Vietnam. This religion was founded by Gautama Siddhartha (c. 563 B.C.–483 B.C.), a prince from the Asian country of Nepal. He taught that humans could end their suffering by giving up desires and achieving Nirvana (bliss or heaven). This was attained by living according to high principles that included using the right words, making the right effort, and taking the right actions. Buddhism gained thousands of followers in Vietnam.

The Chinese may have believed that they were improving Vietnam, but many Vietnamese people disagreed. They did not like interference from a foreign power. The Chinese placed heavy taxes on the peasant farmers. They also prevented the Vietnamese aristocrats, who used to be tax collectors, from carrying out this task and keeping some of the tax money for themselves. Chinese officials collected taxes themselves.

As a result, the Vietnamese began a series of revolts against their Chinese rulers. In the first century A.D., a revolt was led by a Chinese aristocrat named Trung Trac and her sister, Trung Nhi. Unlike most other countries, Vietnam permitted women to hold responsible positions. For a short period, the Trung sisters were successful in driving out the Chinese. Eventually, though, China's superior military power proved to be too much for them. The Trungs were defeated and committed suicide. Two centuries later, another women led a revolt against the Chinese. Her name was Trieu Au. She, too, was defeated and suffered the same fate as the Trungs.

Nevertheless, the Vietnamese revolts continued. In fact, this would remain one of the recurring themes of Vietnamese history. Each time a foreign power came to Vietnam, the people revolted and carried out a war against the invading army. In A.D. 938, a Vietnamese mandarin finally succeeded in defeating the Chinese. His name was Ngo Quyen. He led the Chinese navy into a trap on the Bach Dang River. At low tide, General Ngo had his sailors sink metal spikes into the riverbed. Once the tide rose, the spikes were invisible. Then, Ngo let the Chinese navy chase his own ships along the river. When the tide fell, Ngo Quyen's ships attacked. The Chinese ships sailed over the spikes, and the hulls of their ships were torn to pieces.

For several centuries, Vietnam remained independent. Still, the Chinese regularly tried to take back control of the

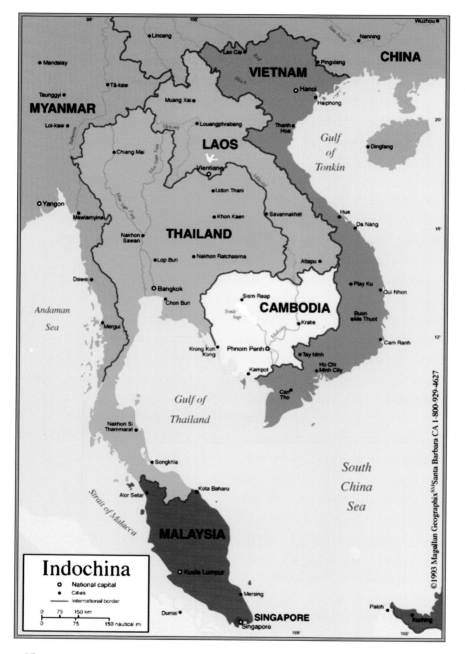

Vietnam occupies the long stretch of Indochina's eastern coast. Its location made it accessible to many foreign visitors, including Indians and Chinese, who greatly influenced Vietnamese culture.

country. In the thirteenth century, the Mongol leader Genghis Khan invaded northern China. His army consisted of mounted horsemen who were considered the greatest cavalry in the world. In 1214, he captured the capital at Chung-tu and took over the area. Meanwhile, Genghis Khan also led his cavalry westward. He carved out a great empire that included much of Russia and the Middle East. Following his death in 1227, the Mongols continued to expand their empire. In 1260, Kublai Khan became emperor of the Mongols. He ruled the empire from a great city called Khanbalig, which is near the present Chinese capital of Beijing. One of the great Khan's visitors was a Venetian merchant named Marco Polo. He described the emperor's great palace in his book, *A Description of the World*. The palace was surrounded by a series of thick walls for defense. The gates were closely guarded by the emperor's soldiers. At the center of this fortress sat a magnificent palace. "The roof is very lofty," Marco Polo wrote, "and the walls of the Palace are all covered with gold and silver. They are also adorned with representations of dragons, beasts and birds, knights and idols. . . . And on the ceiling too you see nothing but gold and silver painting . . . no man on earth could design anything superior to it."

Kublai Khan was not content to rule northern China alone. During the 1260s, he began an invasion of the south. Eventually, he captured all the major cities, and he took complete control of the country by 1280. Then the Mongols turned south and tried to conquer Vietnam. Here, they met stiff opposition led by General Tran Hung Dao. Using guerrilla warfare, he kept the much larger Mongol army off balance. Finally, they were weak enough for Tran Hung Dao to risk a major battle. He defeated the Mongols along the Red River Valley in 1287 and drove them northward. A poem written at the time stated that "this ancient land shall live forever."

While the Vietnamese were dealing with China, they were also trying to expand their own territory. In the south, they attacked the kingdom of Champa. After several centuries of sporadic fighting, Champa was finally conquered in the fifteenth century. While the Vietnamese were focused on the war in the south, however, their country was invaded by China once again. The Chinese overwhelmed the Vietnamese troops and took control of the country. China showed no mercy this time. The Vietnamese people were enslaved and forced to be part of Chinese work gangs in mines and farms. The period of Chinese rule was brief, though. A new Vietnamese leader named Le Loi led a revolt against the Chinese. At first, he used guerrilla tactics. Then, in 1426, he met the Chinese in a major battle. Le Loi used elephants to charge the Chinese cavalry and frighten their horses. The strategy worked, and the Chinese were forced to leave Vietnam. As one poet wrote:

> Henceforth our country is safe.
> Our mountains and rivers begin life afresh.
> Peace follows war as day follows night.
> We have purged shame for a thousand centuries,
> We have regained tranquility for ten thousand generations.

Le Loi ran the country as emperor from Dong Kinh, the present city of Hanoi. He and his followers gave additional land to poor farmers. They also improved the operations of the government so it would be more responsive to the people. Le Loi introduced teams of inspectors who toured the country to make sure local administrations were run fairly. In addition, a large, well-trained army was established to defend Vietnam against invasion.

This army did not protect the country from threats inside Vietnam, however. During the sixteenth century, Vietnam was torn apart by a civil war. The conflict was between an aristocratic family in the north called the Trinh, and the Nguyen, who controlled the central and southern parts of the country. At the same time that this civil war was being fought, Vietnam also faced a new menace: Europeans began to arrive off the Vietnamese coast.

Indochina was a rich source of spices. These included pepper and cloves that were used to preserve food. During the Middle Ages, there was no way to keep food cold until it could be eaten. Therefore, everyone had to rely on spices that could be used as preservatives. One of the most important of these was salt. Venice, a wealthy city on the east coast of Italy, controlled large salt deposits. The Venetians traded their salt for other products in the Mediterranean and the East. Gradually, the Venetian traders established routes that took them across the Middle East to Asia. Here, they traded for other spices, as well as rich silks that were produced in China. Among the most famous of these traders was Marco Polo, who visited Kublai Khan. The Polo family had a trading station in Constantinople (now Istanbul, Turkey), a large city south of the Black Sea. They brought their trade goods there from China. Then they sailed back to Venice, where the trade goods were sold at large profits. During their visit with Kublai Khan, for example, the Polos received priceless jewels, which they sold back in Europe.

For many years, Italian cities such as Venice, Genoa, and Florence controlled these trade routes. There were other nations, however, that wanted to take over these routes for themselves. In Portugal, Prince Henry the Navigator led the effort to start a new route. Henry was a son of the king, John I. He established a base at Sagres in 1416. From Henry's base, explorers began to sail along the coast of Africa. They traded in gold and slaves. Although Henry died in 1460, these explorations continued. In 1498, the Portuguese explorer Vasco da Gama sailed around Africa to the Far East. He had charted a sea route to the Orient that would replace the land route controlled by Venice and other Italian cities. Soon, Portuguese ships were sailing toward Vietnam. In

1535, Portuguese explorers established a base at Faifo, not far from the modern city of Da Nang in central Vietnam. Soon, the Portuguese were followed by other European merchants, including the Dutch, the English, and the French.

In the meantime, Vietnam was still in the middle of a civil war that had begun earlier in the sixteenth century. The Trinh in the north and the Nguyen in the south were continuing to fight for control of the country. The civil war made trading in Vietnam very difficult. Eventually, all the European traders but the Portuguese decided to concentrate their efforts in other areas, such as India and Sri Lanka. The Portuguese traders, on the other hand, not only remained in Vietnam, but they also brought with them Catholic priests. Among these were orders of priests called Jesuits and Franciscans. The Society of Jesus, as the Jesuits were called, had been founded by St. Ignatius of Loyola in 1540. The Jesuits served as missionaries as well as teachers in medieval universities. Some were even advisors to kings. The Franciscans were founded by St. Francis of Assisi in 1209. They were missionaries who were devoted to helping the poor and spreading the teachings of Christianity.

One of the missionaries who came to Vietnam was a French Jesuit named Alexandre de Rhodes. He arrived in 1627 from the Jesuit base in Macao, a Portuguese colony. With his knowledge of the Vietnamese language, he soon impressed the Trinh emperor in Hanoi. The emperor's advisors were fearful of Christianity, however. They believed that Christians cared more about Jesus Christ than they did about the emperor. They worried that the Christians would eventually undermine the emperor's power. Rhodes was driven out of Vietnam by loyal followers of the emperor in 1630, but he continued to return and preach the Christian gospels.

Meanwhile, the Portuguese power was declining in the Far East. France was becoming the stronger military power. The French had far more financial resources to equip a much

King Louis XVI of France supported missionary Pigneau de Behaine's idea to help restore the Vietnamese emperor to his throne. Before Louis could carry out the plan, however, he was deposed by revolutionaries.

larger navy. Rhodes eventually went to France to ask the government of King Louis XIV to help spread Christianity in Vietnam. Although Rhodes died in 1664, the French made a commitment after his death to spread trade and Christianity to the Far East. Little could be done for more than 100 years, however, because the civil war between the Nguyen and the Trinh families continued to tear apart Vietnam.

In the 1770s, the Nguyen family was overthrown in central Vietnam. One member of the family, Nguyen Anh, escaped to a missionary center on the island of Phu Quoc, off the coast of Indochina. There, he was protected by Pigneau de Behaine, the French priest who ran the center. Pigneau went back to France in 1787 to ask Louis XVI to help put

Ngyuen Anh back on the throne. Eventually, Louis agreed. Before a military force could be put together, though, Louis himself was overthrown during the French Revolution.

Pigneau went to India, where the French had trading stations, and received help from the French merchants there. They expected to grow rich if a spice trade could be established with Vietnam. By 1802, the French had succeeded in helping Nguyen Anh regain his throne. The new king called himself Gia Long. His forces had not only taken control of the south, but also the north. He united the country under one ruler, and named it Vietnam.

Although Gia Long realized that he could not have gained power without the help of France, he still mistrusted the Europeans. He was afraid that they might try to take over his country. He also feared that they might be assisted by the Christian missionaries. Therefore, he did nothing to increase the number of missions in Vietnam. He successors went even further. They actively tried to prevent any more missionaries from coming to Vietnam. As the emperors put it, "the perverse religion of the Europeans corrupts the hearts of men." Emperor Minh Mang (ruled 1820–1841), believing that priests had been involved in a plot to overthrow him, wanted the clergymen arrested. Most escaped before his police could catch them.

After the death of Minh Mang, Emperor Thieu Tri continued to oppose Christianity. France retaliated by sending a fleet to the waters off Southeast Asia. In 1847, the French fleet arrived near Tourane in central Vietnam. The fleet's mission was to rescue a French missionary named Dominique Lefebvre, who had been imprisoned by Thieu Tri. Unknown to the French, the missionary had already been released. French ships bombed the harbor at Tourane anyway, and destroyed it.

In 1847, an emperor named Tu Duc ascended the Vietnamese throne. He decided that the time had come to drive out the Christians from Vietnam and to kill all their priests. Two French priests were killed in 1851. France now believed it was time to take action against the Vietnamese government. The new French emperor, Louis Napoleon, wanted to expand the power of France. As the nephew of Napoleon Bonaparte, he wanted to see the country achieve the glory it had enjoyed under his uncle's reign. At that time, France had controlled a great empire that stretched across much of Europe. The stage was now set for France to try to take control of Vietnam and make it part of a new French empire.

Charles Louis Napoleon Bonaparte was emperor of France from 1852 to 1871. He had a strong desire to expand his empire as much as possible and this goal led him to increase French power over Vietnam.

Conquest by France

In 1858, a war fleet made up of about a dozen ships steamed toward Tourane. Emperor Louis Napoleon had decided to expand French power over Vietnam. He was also concerned that the Vietnamese emperor, Tu Doc, might kill more Christians in the country.

The French force was commanded by Admiral Charles Rigault de Genouilly, who had participated in the bombing of Tourane 11 years earlier. In addition to the ships, the admiral's force included more than 2,000 French soldiers whose mission was to take control of Tourane. When the French arrived, they had no trouble overwhelming Tourane's few defenders and capturing the city. There were not enough French troops to push out into the countryside and take over the area around Tourane, however. Instead, the French were trapped inside the city, while outside Vietnamese guerrilla forces held on to the surrounding country.

Rigault de Genouilly realized that he could not change the situation, so he took part of his forces and sailed south. Traveling inland, he attacked the city of Saigon. It was located on the Mekong River, a rich rice-growing area. Saigon fell to the French in early 1859. Once again, though, the French were unable to expand their control of the area because of Vietnamese guerrilla forces. Rigault de Genouilly knew he did not have enough troops to occupy both positions. Tourane was abandoned.

Meanwhile, a French relief force had reinforced the troops in Saigon. With fresh soldiers, the French were successful in expanding their control of the Mekong River Delta. Emperor Tu Duc finally decided to sign a peace treaty with the French. The Vietnamese king realized that he was too weak to hold the southern part of the country. Therefore, he turned over the area around Saigon to France.

In the south, French forces strengthened their position. Nevertheless, they were constantly forced to fight the Vietnamese guerrillas, who were no more eager to let France into Vietnam than earlier generations of guerrillas had been willing to accept Chinese control. Once again, the Vietnamese resorted to their age-old custom of resisting invaders. The French were too powerful to be stopped, however. They not only remained in control of the area around Saigon, but also invaded the neighboring country of Cambodia. There, they forced the weak king to give up his country to France.

In the north, the monarchy of Tu Doc was also unable to withstand the power of the French. In 1873, a French merchant named Jean Dupuis decided that the only way to protect his trading interests in Hanoi was to have France take over the city. At first, Dupuis acted on his own. He and his employees took control of one part of the city. Then they asked the French forces in Saigon to march north and capture all of Hanoi. Once a French relief force arrived, it took not only Hanoi but the surrounding countryside as well. Occupying the area and holding it were two different things, though. Vietnamese guerrillas attacked the French and successfully drove them back into Hanoi.

In 1873, Emperor Tu Doc and the French decided to sign another treaty. France realized that it could not control the entire country. Therefore, the French agreed to give up the north. Tu Doc granted them complete control of the south. Despite the treaty, the French did not give up on their efforts to retake the north. During the early 1880s, they returned to the area outside Hanoi and tried to take control of it again. They were defeated once more by the Vietnamese guerrillas.

In 1883, Emperor Tu Doc died. The Vietnamese government was left without a leader strong enough to withstand the power of the French. That same year, French forces attacked the Vietnamese capital at Hue. This city is located on the Perfume River in central Vietnam. Vietnamese government leaders agreed to turn over their country to France. The new emperor, Ham Nghi, however, resisted this decision. French troops retaliated. Led by General Roussell de Courcy, French troops destroyed part of Hue. Ham Nghi quickly left Vietnam, leaving the French as the rulers of Vietnam. The French appointed another Vietnamese ruler, Dong Khanh, who was also a member of the Vietnamese royal family. By 1887, they had established an empire in French Indochina that included Vietnam, Cambodia, and later Laos.

The creation of the French empire in Southeast Asia was part of nineteenth-century imperialism. *Imperialism* referred to efforts by European countries to carve out empires in Africa and Asia. Nations such as France, England, Germany, and Belgium took over huge territories. There were several reasons behind European imperialism. The nations of Europe wanted the natural resources that could be found in Africa and Asia. For example, in the Congo region of southern Africa, Belgium took over an area that was rich in rubber. The Belgians used this rubber to make tires for bicycles, and later, automobiles. Empires also created new markets for European manufactured goods. The European empire-builders tried to prevent any domestic manufacturing from developing in the areas they conquered. That left them with a big market in which they could sell items produced in their own countries to African and Asian peoples. The British, for example, discouraged the production of cotton clothing in India so that their merchants could sell English-made clothes to the Indian people.

Another reason for imperialism was a desire by the Europeans to spread their culture to other parts of the world. They believed that European cultures and the Christian religion were superior to the local customs of Africa and Asia. The Europeans claimed that it was their job—"the white man's burden"—to bring the advantages of their society to Africans and Asians. During the late nineteenth century, many European missionaries set off for Africa and Asia to teach Christianity to the native peoples. The Europeans did not seem to appreciate that these people already had their own deeply held religious beliefs, including Hinduism and Buddhism.

One other reason for imperialism was a fear in each European country that, if its armies did not occupy a certain area, another country might grab it. The French, for example, were afraid that if they did not take over Vietnam, it might fall to another European nation. Vietnam had rich coal mines that provided a source of fuel for ships. The French did not want any rival to gain access to this coal and prevent France's navy from using it.

Once the French took control of Vietnam, they quickly established colonial rule. Vietnam was broken up into three colonies. In the north was Tonkin, which included the city of Hanoi. Annam was in the center, where Tourane (or Da Nang) was located. In the south was Cochin China, which included Saigon. The French allowed the Vietnamese emperor to remain in power. This gave the French legitimacy—that is, more people were willing to accept the foreign rule because they respected the authority of the emperor. The Vietnamese emperor had no power, though. France ruled Vietnam through a small number of bureaucrats sent from Paris to govern the country. These officials were not fluent in Vietnamese, however. Nor did they understand the customs of the people. Therefore, the French had to depend on local officials, called interpreters or culture brokers, to help run the country at the local level.

Once the French had established their rule, they made numerous changes in Vietnam. In the past, Vietnamese peasants had worked their own plots of land. The French took many of these plots and consolidated them into large landholdings. They were often helped by the local culture brokers and Vietnamese aristocrats. These people frequently used their knowledge of the law to steal land from the peasants and create huge estates for themselves. Eventually, in Tonkin, approximately 900 landowners controlled over half of the farmland.

Through improved methods of irrigation, the French greatly increased the amount of rice produced in Vietnam. Instead of using it to feed the Vietnamese, however, the French exported it to other parts of the world. Vietnam also became a rich rubber-producing area, after the French introduced rubber trees. Vietnamese laborers were forced to work on huge French rubber plantations along the border with Cambodia. Many Vietnamese workers died from disease or because they were poorly fed. Instead of using the rubber to produce finished goods in Vietnam, most of the rubber was exported. The

The Culture Brokers

The Vietnamese culture brokers became very powerful during the years of French rule. They served as tax collectors and village mayors. Peasant farmers went to the culture brokers if they had a problem. These officials were expected to deal with the problem themselves or report it to the French bureaucrats to be resolved.

Many culture brokers were very corrupt. In one province, for example, a culture broker "had given peasants tax receipts for amounts far less than they had actually paid and had pocketed the difference. [Using local peasants] . . . , he had built ten guard-houses on his own property. For guards he had recruited the local militia, paid from the public treasury."

Since the peasants respected the local culture broker, they did whatever he wanted. Often, he was the only person in a village who could read or write. He alone understood both French and the Vietnamese language. Therefore, only he could carry out all the official French policies that affected the Vietnamese people. This gave him enormous power. The French were content to let the culture brokers control Vietnam locally. Meanwhile, most French officials and their families stayed in the major cities. Here, they tried to re-create the culture and lifestyle they had known back in France. French restaurants, shops, and theaters sprung up to satisfy the tastes of the bureaucrats. Few bureaucrats ever tried to absorb the culture of Vietnam.

Soon after they had secured their rule in Vietnam, the French began to mistreat the native people. For example, Vietnamese laborers were forced to do grueling work on rubber plantations such as this one.

country only had two rubber-processing factories. The French also improved the coal industry in Vietnam with modern mining methods. Still, the Vietnamese miners were paid very low wages, which amounted to no more than 25 cents per day. Most of the mining was controlled by a small number of French companies.

In addition to controlling Vietnam's natural resources, the French took charge of other parts of the economy. In 1897, Paul Doumer became governor-general of French Indochina. One of the economic changes he made was to give the French government complete control of all the opium, alcohol, and salt produced in the country. Opium is a strong narcotic produced from the seed capsules of poppy plants grown in Southeast Asia. Some Vietnamese were already addicted to opium. "Doumer built a refinery in Saigon. . . . Vietnamese addiction soon rose so sharply that opium eventually accounted for one third of the colonial administration's income." The French also collected large sums of money by controlling the sale of alcohol, which the Vietnamese drank, and salt, which was used to preserve food.

The Vietnamese were no happier under French rule than they had been under Chinese rule centuries earlier. The Vietnamese responded in the same way: with revolts and guerrilla warfare. At first, opposition to French rule was led by former Vietnamese Emperor Ham Nghi. The rebellion was called the "Scholars' Revolt" because it received support from many well-educated Vietnamese who had served as officials in the government. The revolt continued for about ten years until the late 1890s. The guerrillas had some early success in attacking French outposts. The French had strong support from many aristocratic landowners and culture brokers who had benefited from French rule, however. The French and their allies used brutal methods to put down the revolts. They sometimes destroyed entire villages where peasants had sheltered the rebels. Eventually, Ham Nghi was captured by the French and exiled from Vietnam.

Even without him, the guerrilla movement continued. Finally, the French besieged the guerrillas in their mountain camps. To defeat the enemy, the guerrillas launched an attack on the French troops. The Europeans' superior firepower destroyed the guerrilla army and brought a temporary end to the rebel movement. In 1907, however, another revolt broke out. This one was led by a mandarin named Phan Boi Chau. Phan had developed a plot to poison a number of French military officers. They were to be killed by the Vietnamese soldiers who served under them. The regular Vietnamese army consisted of about 30,000 soldiers. Of these, 10,000 were French officers. Although many officers were poisoned, none died. Meanwhile, peasant farmers had begun to demonstrate against the French government. Some even came to the city of Hue to protest. Phan hoped that a rebellion would break out across Vietnam. But it never occurred. Phan had never been able to win broad support among the poor. His rebellion was supported almost entirely by the educated Vietnamese and some business owners. There were not enough of them to lead a successful revolt. Phan Boi Chau was captured and put into prison.

One rebel leader who worked with Phan was Phan Chu Trinh. Like Phan Boi Chau, he was a mandarin trained to serve in the government. Phan realized that he could not work for the French. He believed they had imposed an unfair rule on the country, and he called on the French governor to reform the government. Phan wanted the French to bring democracy to Vietnam. He also demanded that the French industrialize the country, reduce taxes on peasant farmers, and expand education for the Vietnamese. At that time, most Vietnamese people could not read or write. No more than a handful attended the University at Hanoi, the only college in Vietnam.

Although the French brought many improvements to Vietnam, few native people reaped the benefits of these advances. For the most part, the people remained poor and uneducated, particularly in regard to higher education. Vietnam had only one college, the University of Indochina (shown here), and it was attended by a very small number of Vietnamese students.

The French had no intention of doing what Phan asked. Instead, they arrested him in 1908, after the plot against the French officers had failed. Although Phan was tried and sentenced to be executed, the French decided to keep him in prison. Eventually, Phan was exiled from Vietnam and went to live in France. From Paris, he continued to support the Vietnamese revolution. In France, he attracted a group of Vietnamese followers who had fled the country. Among them was a young scholar named Nguyen Sinh Cung, who would go on to transform the history of Vietnam.

General Vo Nguyen Giap was the talented Viet Minh leader who turned a largely disorganized collection of guerrilla fighters into an army powerful enough to defeat the French and their superior weapons.

4

Nguyen Sinh Cung (Ho Chi Minh)

Nguyen Sinh Cung was born on May 19, 1890, in the province of Nghe An, in central Vietnam. While he was a child, Cung's father, Nguyen Sinh Sac, taught school and studied for the examinations required to enter the government civil service. In 1894, Nguyen Sinh Sac passed the exams and eventually received a position with the government. Tragedy soon struck the family, however. Early in 1901, Cung's mother, Hoang Thi Loan, died while giving birth to Cung's brother. Sac left government service and opened a school in a local village. There, he raised his three sons and one daughter.

Among the visitors to Nguyen Sinh Sac's school was Sac's old friend, the Vietnamese patriot Phan Boi Chau. Sac supported Vietnamese independence and saw the French occupation of his country as a terrible blow to the future of his people. Although the government wanted him to return to civil service, Nguyen Sinh Sac refused for a time. He could not bring himself to serve the French. The pressure on him eventually became too great, though. In 1906, he traveled with his two oldest sons to the imperial capital at Hue where he took a new position with the government. His sons went to school in the city. After graduation from elementary school, Cung entered the National Academy, similar to a secondary school, in 1907.

While Cung attended school, a revolt broke out in Vietnam—Phan Boi Chau's plot to poison French officers and overthrow the government. Cung supported his father's old friend. When peasant crowds marched on the capital in 1908, Cung joined them. For this, he was punished by the French government. Police arrived at his school one morning and asked to see him immediately. They entered his class, and one of them told his teacher: "I have orders to request that this troublemaker be dismissed from school." Cung was expelled.

Cung headed south, away from Hue. He found a job as a teacher in southern Vietnam, using an assumed name, Nguyen Tat Thanh. The French police kept him under constant watch. Eventually, Thanh left the school, and in 1911, took a job aboard a ship that was sailing from Saigon. Over the next several years, he traveled the oceans of the world. Thanh's voyages took him to France, India, to the seaports of many African countries, and to New York City. By 1914, Thanh was in London, working in a luxury hotel. Three years later, he had left the British capital and traveled to Paris.

In 1917, Paris was home to a fairly large Vietnamese community. Some Vietnamese had come to Paris to study.

Others had left home because of their revolutionary activities. Among these people was the patriot Phan Chu Trinh, who ran a photography shop. Phan gave Thanh a job. While he lived in Paris, Thanh attended meetings of the French Socialist Party. Then, in 1919, he started his own organization. It was called the Association of Annamite Patriots. Thanh had grown up in Annam, in central Vietnam. The purpose of Thanh's group was to build opposition to French control of Indochina. As head of the organization, Thanh became a leader among the Vietnamese in Paris. He spoke to Vietnamese workers and encouraged them to demand better wages in French factories.

In 1919, after the end of World War I, a peace conference was held in France. The meeting took place at Versailles, outside Paris, which had been a magnificent palace built by King Louis XIV in the seventeenth century. Among the leaders attending the conference was U.S. President Woodrow Wilson. Wilson was asking the world to begin a new era of peace built on his so-called Fourteen Points. His plan included a League of Nations—an organization dedicated to preventing war. Wilson also called for colonial empires to end and for every people to be allowed to determine its own future.

Thanh believed that the time had come to express his belief in Vietnamese freedom. As a Vietnamese leader in Paris, he prepared a list of grievances against French rule in Indochina. In a manifesto presented to the leaders meeting at Versailles, Thanh asked that the Vietnamese be given the opportunity to enjoy freedom of speech and the press and freedom of religion. He also requested an end to the French monopolies on salt, opium, and alcohol. He signed his manifesto, *Nguyen Ai Quoc*, which meant "Nguyen the Patriot." This became his new name.

The manifesto alerted the French police to his revolutionary viewpoint and officers began to follow him. Eventually, the police realized that Nguyen Ai Quoc was the same Nguyen Sinh Cung who had been expelled from the academy at Hue for revolutionary activities. Nevertheless, Nguyen Ai Quoc was allowed to remain in France.

While he had been living in Paris, a successful revolution had occurred in Russia. The autocratic government of the tsars (Russian rulers) had been overthrown. In its place arose a Communist government run by Vladimir Ilyich Lenin, who renamed Russia the Union of Soviet Socialist Republics (Soviet Union, or USSR). The new Soviet Union was admired by many people. The Russian Communists had replaced an autocratic government in Russia. Other oppressed peoples believed that communism might be an alternative to the colonial empires and autocratic governments that controlled much of Africa and Asia. Communist parties began to spring up in other parts of the world. In 1921, Nguyen Ai Quoc joined the French Communist Party (FCP).

Nguyen Ai Quoc wrote articles praising communism and calling for an end to the French colonial empire. He believed that communism might offer his people an opportunity to become independent. He rose to become the most important Vietnamese member of the FCP. His name came to the attention of the Communist leaders in the Soviet Union. They were looking for someone to help them increase their influence in Southeast Asia. In 1923, the Soviet government invited Nguyen Ai Quoc to go to Moscow, the capital of the Soviet Union, to study and work.

In Moscow, Nguyen Ai Quoc studied at the Communist University of the Toilers of the East. He also worked in the government, helping to spread the message of communism

In 1917, revolutionaries in Russia successfully overthrew the tsar, took over the government, and installed a new communist system. Their success made Vietnamese rebels, such as Ho Chi Minh, view communism as a good option to replace French rule in Vietnam.

to Southeast Asia. He repeatedly reminded the Communist leaders that they had a great chance to gain followers in Asia, where many people suffered under the colonial governments. As he told one meeting of Communist leaders:

"In all the French colonies, famine is on the increase and so is the people's hatred. The native peasants are ripe for insurrection. . . . [We] must help them to revolution and liberation."

In 1924, the Soviet government ordered Nguyen Ai Quoc to go to China. From a base in Canton, he was supposed to work with revolutionaries in southeast Asia to bring an end to French colonialism in Indochina. The Chinese emperor had been overthrown in a revolution during 1911. A new president, Dr. Sun Yat-sen, was leading a national government in the southern part of China. Along with another Chinese leader, Chiang Kai-Shek, Sun tried to expand the government's control in the north. Eventually, Sun made an alliance with Soviet leaders to assist him.

Nguyen Ai Qoc's goal was to start a new revolutionary party in Vietnam. Its mission would be to lead a rebellion against the French colonial administration and over-throw it. He realized that this effort might take a long time, though. In 1925, he took the first step—he established the Vietnamese Revolutionary Youth League. Then he brought young Vietnamese to Canton to train them in Communist principles and revolutionary tactics. There were already young, educated members of the Vietnamese middle class who had grown tired of French rule. They saw that most good jobs or high positions in the government were open only to French immigrants, not native Vietnamese. Indeed, during the 1920s, only about 5,000 Vietnamese even graduated from high school. Much of the fertile land in Vietnam was owned by the French, while more than 500,000 peasants had no land at all.

Nguyen Ai Quoc used the alias Vuong to hide his true identity while he taught the students who came to school in Canton. He "was the most popular teacher in the

Dr. Sun Yat-sen, seen here in a 1922 photograph, became the nationalist president of south China after the overthrow of the Chinese emperor in 1911. It was during his time in office that Nguyen Ai Quoc carried out revolutionary activities in China under the command of the Soviet Union.

school. They [the students] remembered him as slender with bright eyes and a warm voice, friendly and good-humored, although he rarely laughed. Vuong was exceptionally approachable and patient with his students." In addition to teaching, Nguyen Ai Quoc published material about the best ways to start a revolution. He emphasized that the mass of peasants must be involved in a rebellion in order for it to be successful.

In 1930, Nguyen Ai Quoc founded the Vietnamese Communist Party. (It was later named the Indochinese Communist Party.) By this time, the world had slid into a widespread and severe economic depression. Conditions inside Vietnam had grown steadily worse. The French had begun to industrialize the country, but wages were very low for Vietnamese working in factories. Then, many workers lost their jobs because of the depression. Strikes broke out during the early 1930s, and were violently put down by the French army. In the meantime, the French monopolies of salt, alcohol, and opium kept prices too high for most Vietnamese to afford. This led many peasant farmers to oppose French rule bitterly.

These poor conditions helped the Communists, who began to infiltrate the factories. They gained the support of workers who were unhappy with the low wages paid by employers. Communists also began to visit peasants in their villages and gather support from people who no longer supported the French government. In some areas, peasants led by the Communists threw out local government officials. As opposition grew, however, the French were not standing by and doing nothing. The army marched in and slaughtered many Vietnamese, including Communists and other rebel leaders. By 1931, more than 50,000 Vietnamese had been thrown into prison.

During this time, Nguyen Ai Quoc had moved his headquarters from China to the British colony of Hong Kong. He was arrested here in 1931. His capture was an effort by the British to do what the French had done in

Indochina—eliminate any Communists who might be planning a revolt. Nguyen Ai Quoc was released by the British the following year, and he returned to Moscow. He remained there for the next six years, training Vietnamese who traveled to the Soviet Union to learn more about communism. In the meantime, the Communist Party in Vietnam was struggling to survive. As its membership grew in the south, crackdowns by the French government occurred in Annam and Tonkin. As a result, Communist activities remained very limited. Finally, in 1938, Nguyen Ai Quoc returned to China.

By this time, China was mired in a bloody war with Japan. During the 1930s, Japan had expanded its power on the continent of Asia. In 1932, the Japanese took control of Manchuria. Then, Japanese military leaders turned their attention south to China. Sun Yat-sen had died in 1925, and he was succeeded by General Chiang Kai-shek. Chiang Kai-shek did not trust the Communists, but he was willing to work with them against the common enemy of Japan. In 1937, the Japanese army had captured Peking and Shanghai in northern China. That same year, they captured Nanking, where they massacred thousands of Chinese people. The following year, the Japanese advanced south and captured Canton, but Chiang Kai-shek continued to fight.

In Vietnam, the Indochinese Communist Party (ICP) tried to attract more supporters, including peasants and factory workers. For a time, Nguyen Ai Quoc remained in China, where he could not be arrested by French authorities. He continued to bring in recruits who wanted to join the ICP. Among these new party members was Vo Nguyen Giap, who would become one of Nguyen Ai Quoc's most valuable associates.

As the training program continued in China, World War II began. In September 1939, Germany's Nazi army invaded Poland. Great Britain and France entered the war to fight against the Nazis. The following year, German dictator Adolf Hitler sent his forces into France, which surrendered to the Germans in June 1940. Nguyen Ai Quoc believed that the fall of France presented an opportunity for him and the Communists. The French might no longer be powerful enough to stop a revolt. In 1941, he crossed the border and returned to Vietnam. At this time, he adopted a new name to keep his identity a secret. He called himself *Ho Chi Minh*, which means "He Who Enlightens." Ho and his associates set up their headquarters at a town in northern Vietnam called Pac Bo. They also established a new group, called the Viet Minh. This organization was designed to bring together all the people who opposed the French government in Vietnam—Communists as well as non-Communists.

Even as the French were dealing with German conquest

Vo Nguyen Giap

Vo Nguyen Giap was born in 1910, 20 years after Nguyen Ai Quoc. His family had participated in the revolt against the French during the later part of the nineteenth century. Like Nguyen Ai Quoc, Giap had attended the National Academy in Hue and was later sent to prison for supporting revolution. Giap was paroled and attended Hanoi University, where he received a law degree. He taught history for a short time and married Nguyen Thi Minh Giang. He then worked as a reporter for the Communist newspaper in Vietnam. Although he had no formal training as a military leader, Giap studied the battles and great generals of the past. In the late 1930s, he went to China to work under Nguyen Ai Quoc. The two men would remain close associates for over three decades. Together, they would wage wars against both France and the United States. Giap eventually became the most successful military leader of the Communist forces in Vietnam.

in Europe, they had to contend with a new enemy in Indochina—Japan. The Japanese army was much too strong for the French colonial soldiers to defeat. By 1941, the Japanese had taken over Vietnam, but left the French in control to run the government. The Japanese were only interested in Vietnam's huge supplies of rice and rubber. They needed the rice to feed their armies and the rubber to make tires for their military vehicles.

The Japanese conquest was a tragedy for Vietnam. So much rice was exported to Japan that the Vietnamese did not have enough left to feed themselves. Despite this hardship, Japanese occupation also presented another opportunity for the Communists. Ho Chi Minh hoped the Vietnamese would hate the Japanese soldiers strongly enough that many would decide to join the Communist movement. Then, if Japan's power began to decline in Indochina, the Communists could launch a revolution and take back Vietnam for the Vietnamese.

In 1941, however, Ho was just beginning his efforts to start a revolution. At his northern base, he taught his supporters the elements of communism and revolution. One of them later recalled: "Hour after hour, seated around the fire, we listened to him, like children listening to a legend." Ho's name was known by many people in Vietnam who wanted to regain control of their country. Early in 1942, Ho and the Communists moved their base farther south into Vietnam. Little by little, more Communist encampments began to spring up in other parts of Vietnam. Even so, Ho knew that a lot more work was necessary before the Viet Minh would be strong enough to take on the Japanese or the French.

In the summer of 1942, Ho returned briefly to China, probably to win support from the Chinese government. At this time, however, Chiang Kai-Shek had apparently decided that Communist leaders could not be trusted as allies. Ho was arrested and put in prison by the Chinese. Fortunately for him, he found himself under the control of a Chinese general, Zhang Fakui, who seemed to support the cause of Vietnamese independence. Zhang believed that the Vietnamese could help China defeat the Japanese. In 1943, Zhang released Ho Chi Minh and let him return to Vietnam.

Over the next two years, the Japanese were steadily pushed back by U.S. forces in the Pacific Ocean. In Europe, the Americans and their fellow Allies invaded France and forced the Nazis eastward toward Germany in 1944. A new democratic government came to power in France. The Japanese feared that this new government would want to change the alliance between Japan and the French colonial government in Indochina. Mistrusting the French, the Japanese took complete control of Indochina in March 1945. The days of Japanese power in Indochina were numbered, however. American forces were slowly advancing against the islands of Japan. Then, in August 1945, the United States dropped atomic bombs on the Japanese cities of Hiroshima and Nagasaki. Shortly afterward, Japan surrendered. Ho Chi Minh and his associates realized that the time was quickly approaching when the Communists might be able to seize power.

Ho Chi Minh recognized that Vietnam was in a state of confusion. With the Japanese surrender, no one was in charge of the country. The time had come to begin a revolt. As Ho announced to the Vietnamese people: "The decisive hour in the destiny of our people has struck. Let us stand up with all our strength to liberate ourselves!" In Vietnam, the Japanese officials realized that they had to leave the country. No sooner had they prepared to depart, than the Viet Minh sprung into action. Under the direction of Communist leaders, they took over the government in

Hanoi, occupying important buildings such as police head-quarters and city hall. Then they raised the Viet Minh flag. After almost a century, Vietnam was about to become an independent nation once again—or so it seemed.

5

The Road to Dien Bien Phu

On September 2, 1945, Ho Chi Minh spoke from Hanoi to the people of Vietnam. As part of his speech, he said, "We hold the truth that all men are created equal, that they are endowed by their Creator with certain unalienable rights, among them life, liberty, and the pursuit of happiness." Ho knew that Americans had used similar words in their own Declaration of Independence in 1776. He hoped that the U.S. government might now support the efforts of Vietnam to become independent, too. Indeed, during World War II, the U.S. army had supplied the Viet Minh with weapons to fight the Japanese.

The Vietnamese were disappointed, however. Several months earlier, U.S. President Harry Truman had met with Allied leaders at Potsdam, Germany, after the surrender of the Nazis. Among other decisions, they had agreed to divide Vietnam in half along the sixteenth parallel of latitude. The Chinese would control the northern section, while the British would take over the south.

Great Britain did not intend to rule the south alone. In fact, the British wanted to return the area to French control. Many Vietnamese were eager for independence, though. When it became clear to the Viet Minh what the Allies intended, they organized large protest demonstrations in Saigon. These were followed by a city-wide strike. The British could not put down the protests, so they called in the French. The French soldiers had been put in prison during the Japanese takeover of Vietnam in 1945. They were set free by the British. In clashes that occurred between French soldiers and the Viet Minh, innocent civilians were brutally killed. Gradually, the French took back control of Saigon.

In the north, meanwhile, Ho Chi Minh faced an invasion by the Chinese forces that entered Hanoi and began to take over the city with an army that was much larger than the Viet Minh. Ho knew he was too weak to set up a new government for an independent Vietnam. Eventually, in 1946, Ho Chi Minh agreed that the French should remain in Vietnam. France was prepared to give the Vietnamese some control over local affairs, but the French would remain in charge of the army. This agreement proved to be just the calm before a great storm. In Hanoi and Haiphong, battles continued to rage between the Viet Minh and the French. Eventually, the Viet Minh were driven out of Hanoi, and by 1947, the French controlled the major cities in Vietnam. In the fall of that year, they launched a major attack against the Viet Minh north of Hanoi. In a surprise attack by French paratroopers, Ho Chi Minh and General Giap were almost captured. As historian Philip Davidson wrote:

> The airborne assault surprised Giap and Ho in their head-
> quarters, and the French had them in their fingertips.
> In fact, the French captured the letters on Ho's desk.
> The two Communist leaders barely had time to jump into
> a camouflaged hole nearby while French paratroopers
> searched the bushes around and over their heads.

Ho and Giap were lucky to escape with their lives, Davidson added. If the French had captured them during this surprise attack, it might have changed the course of history.

France hoped to rule Vietnam through a emperor named Bao Dai. He had no real power, but governed as a figurehead.

Emperor Bao Dai

Bao Dai was born in 1913. He was a direct descendant of the great Vietnamese Emperor Gia Long. When Bao Dai was still a boy, his father died and Bao Dai became king. The French realized that he was too young to rule, however, so he was sent to Paris to be educated. When he was in his twenties, Bao Dai came back to Vietnam, where he hoped to set up a more independent government. The French had no intention of allowing this to happen. During World War II, Bao Dai continued to rule while the Japanese occupied the country. Once Ho Chi Minh announced the independence of Vietnam, Bao Dai hoped to work with the new government. When this did not seem possible, he left the country to live in Hong Kong. This was a British colony near China in Southeast Asia. There, Bao Dai enjoyed the life of a playboy. In 1948, the French met with the former emperor and tried to persuade him to return to Vietnam. He refused, because they would not give the country any real independence. Eventually, he agreed to return in 1949, after the United States promised to give Vietnam financial support. Bao Dai continued to hope that he might one day convince the French to give his government more independence.

After Bao Dai became emperor of Vietnam, he strove to win his country some degree of independence from France. After Ho Chi Minh declared Vietnam's independence, Bao Dai left the country. He was later brought back to serve as a figurehead for the French government that continued to run Vietnam.

Because Vietnam had always been ruled by an emperor, the French hoped Bao Dai would win more support from the Vietnamese people for their government.

With the French in control of the cities, the Viet Minh retreated to the countryside to the north and west of Hanoi. This area is covered with hills and heavy forests that separate Vietnam from neighboring Laos. It is excellent terrain for an army like the Viet Minh to hide from the French. Although the size of both forces was roughly equal in 1947, the French had far more heavy weapons than the

Viet Minh did. Indeed, Ho Chi Minh called the conflict a battle between an elephant and a grasshopper. The French had powerful artillery. Their army could also rely on tanks and planes, which the Viet Minh did not have. Nevertheless, the French weapons were not very effective against an enemy that was hiding in dense forests.

From Viet Minh headquarters north of Hanoi, Giap strengthened the Viet Minh army. He knew it was only a matter of time before the Viet Minh would be involved in a full-scale war with the French. To win that conflict, the army would have to be much stronger. Giap's staff indoctrinated the new soldiers who joined the army to make them completely loyal to the Viet Minh. Although these young men had never studied the history of Vietnam, they were told about its past conflicts against the Chinese and its successful efforts to achieve independence. The new recruits were assured that if they fought bravely, independence could be achieved again.

The soldiers were organized into three-man cells. These cells became their new family. Each day, the three men would discuss what happened to them and share their attitudes about the coming battles against the French. If one of them hesitated to reveal his thoughts, he knew he would be reported to a more senior Viet Minh official, so most men talked openly. In this way, the loyalty and unity of the army was kept strong.

Meanwhile, Giap ordered that small factories be built in the forests. These plants began to produce hand grenades, bullets, and even machine guns for the Viet Minh soldiers. Most of the roads throughout Vietnam were rough and narrow. Therefore, it was difficult to supply an army as it marched. In addition, the Viet Minh did not have enough vehicles to support their troops. To deal with these problems, Giap put together a large group of porters who could carry food and ammunition for the army over long distances. These porters would be able to walk in places where the roads were too rough for vehicles to pass.

In 1950, Giap decided that his army was powerful enough to launch a full-scale attack. The new Communist government, led by Mao Zedong, offered the Viet Minh a source of supplies, including food and ammunition. In addition, if the Viet Minh were pushed back by the French, they could retreat into China and find safety from the enemy. Giap's targets were a series of French posts, or forts, that were spread across the northern border of Vietnam. Giap was especially eager to remove this area from French control. China had been taken over by Communists in late 1949.

Giap began his campaign in September 1950, at the end of the summer rainy season, or monsoon, in Vietnam. From May until September, Vietnam faces a deluge of heavy rains that made a military campaign almost impossible. An army cannot move very easily through the heavy downpours and the thick mud. Once the rainy season was over, however, Giap was ready to strike. He placed his artillery in the hills surrounding a fort called Dong Khe. After bombarding the fort, he sent in his infantry who were too strong for the French defenders to fight off. After the fall of Dong Khe, Giap successfully attacked the other French forts north of Hanoi. All of them had fallen to the Viet Minh by the end of 1950.

The French realized that they faced a major crisis in Vietnam. The Communists had proven that they could carry out and win a major military campaign. To counter Giap, the French sent a new commander to Vietnam. His name was Jean de Lattre de Tassigny. He gradually devised a new strategy to halt the Viet Minh advances.

Giap believed the time had come to lead the Viet Minh on an assault against French positions around Hanoi. He had not considered the abilities of de Lattre, however. In one battle, the Viet Minh attacks were repelled by French air power. As historian Phillip B. Davidson explained, "The French air force used every plane available . . . and

General Jean de Lattre de Tassigny came to Vietnam to help the French set up better defenses against the increasingly powerful Viet Minh. Although his strategy showed promise, he was unable to complete his work. He became very ill and had to leave Vietnam.

poured napalm [fire bombs] . . . and gunfire with brutal effectiveness into the massed Vietminh attackers. Under the flaming napalm the Vietminh panicked and ran screaming back into the forest from which they had come."

Despite his success, de Lattre realized that this would not be enough to achieve victory. To defend the area around Hanoi, he began to build a series of 1,200 of small posts. These were called the "de Lattre Line." The posts were relatively close together. That meant that, if one were attacked, the men in the other nearby posts could help their comrades. General de Lattre hoped to train Vietnamese who were loyal to the French to defend this line. Many Vietnamese did not support the Communists, including large landowners who had grown wealthy under the French as well as others who did not trust Ho Chi Minh and his associates. De Lattre expected that these people could defend Hanoi while his own troops went on the offensive against the Viet Minh.

During General de Lattre's command of French forces, by the end of 1951, Viet Minh control of the countryside around Hanoi was reduced. The Viet Minh still commanded much of the area, though. The French did not have enough manpower to attack and push out the Viet Minh. The French also had another problem. General de Lattre had come down with cancer. He had to leave Vietnam, and died in early 1952.

General Giap realized that the best way to wage war against the French was to draw them away from Hanoi. The defensive line there was too tough to crack. In addition, French planes could easily defend the area from nearby airfields. The French had also placed gunboats

Jean de Lattre de Tassigny

*D*e Lattre was born in 1889 in the western part of France. He attended the French military academy at Saint Cyr and fought during World War I. De Lattre served in the trenches along the Western Front, where French and British soldiers fought German soldiers in bloody battles in which thousands of soldiers died to gain only a few yards of ground. In battles such as Verdun in 1916, de Lattre was wounded several times. Still, he repeatedly returned to the front lines to lead his men, and he received numerous medals for bravery. After World War I, de Lattre remained in the army. When World War II broke out in 1939, he led his infantry division in the defense of France against the invading Nazis. After the fall of France in 1940, de Lattre was put in prison. He escaped and went to North Africa late in 1943. The following year, he led one of the Allied armies that invaded Europe. For the rest of the war, he led them across western Europe into Germany. De Lattre was an inspirational leader who was widely respected by his men. The French considered him one of their finest generals. He was a logical choice to go to Vietnam to save the French armies from defeat by the Viet Minh.

along the rivers between Hanoi and the coast of Vietnam, as well as along the coast itself, to bombard Viet Minh troops operating in the area. By this time, France was also receiving substantial financial aid from the United States.

The government of President Truman regarded Vietnam as a key element in the U.S. policy of containment. With the support of its allies, the United States hoped to keep communism contained within certain defined areas. These included Eastern Europe, which had already been taken over by the Soviet Union, and China. U.S. officials feared that, if Vietnam fell to Communist forces under Ho Chi Minh, Chinese influence would expand into Southeast Asia. Eventually, U.S. officials feared, the Chinese might extend their control over Laos, Cambodia, and Thailand. Indeed, China was already assisting Ho Chi Minh in training the Viet Minh soldiers. Over the next few years, U.S. aid to France increased until, by 1954, the American government was financing approximately 80 percent of the French war effort.

During 1952, General Giap tried to lure the French out of their strongholds around Hanoi. He attacked positions north and west of the city. One of these positions was a French post near Laos called Dien Bien Phu, which was taken over by the Viet Minh. Giap had decided to invade Laos, which was also part of the French empire. It was defended by a small force of French troops and Laotians. In response, the French launched an attack northward to cut off Giap's supply routes into Laos. This campaign failed, and Giap continued his advance into Laos. By the spring of 1953, he was threatening to capture several major Laotian cities, including Luang Prabang and Vientiane. The French rushed in reinforcements by air to Luang Prabang, and the Viet Minh retreated.

Giap headed back eastward to Vietnam. Despite this setback, the Viet Minh retained control of Dien Bien Phu. This would lead to a great siege to decide the fate of the French empire in Indochina.

The rough jungle terrain of Dien Bien Phu made fighting difficult for the French forces, who were used to traditional battlefields. For the Viet Minh, on the other hand, the thick foliage and frequent heavy mist made the area perfect for carrying out the kind of guerrilla attacks they did best.

The Siege Begins

*D*ien Bien Phu lies in a fertile rice-growing area in the highlands of northwestern Vietnam. The name Dien Bien Phu means "big administrative center on the frontier." It is a flat area, 3 miles (5 kilometers) wide and 11 miles (18 kilometers) long, and it has an airfield. Surrounding this flat area are hills covered by dense forests. The French regarded Dien Bien Phu as an important stronghold from which they could launch attacks against the Viet Minh if they invaded Laos. Dien Bien Phu's airfield, the French reasoned, would allow them to easily supply an army in the area.

Although the Viet Minh had easily captured Dien Bien Phu in 1952, they held it with only a small contingent of soldiers. The

French quickly began to make plans to recapture it. In the spring of 1953, a new commander, General Henri Navarre, took over the French forces in Indochina. At 55 years old, Navarre was a veteran of World War I and had led a regiment of tanks across Europe into Germany during World War II. He was a seasoned soldier, but he had no experience fighting in Indochina.

Navarre recognized that the French faced serious problems in Vietnam. Although his French forces controlled the major cities, the Viet Minh still operated freely throughout much of the countryside. There was very little that the French could do to stop them. Navarre decided to launch hit-and-run attacks with French paratroopers. He attacked a Viet Minh supply depot near the Chinese border. Then he struck at the Viet Minh in central Vietnam. He also decided that Laos had to be defended in case the Viet Minh decided to launch another assault there. So, in July, he began preparations to reoccupy Dien Bien Phu if it looked as if the Communists were going to invade Laos again.

General Navarre's staff had mixed feelings about sending French soldiers to Dien Bien Phu. Some of Navarre's subordinates believed the position was far too dangerous. If the Viet Minh could bring a large force to the area and put their artillery on the hills, a French army might be trapped. Other staff members disagreed. They pointed out that the Viet Minh were incapable of concentrating such a large force in one area. They lacked the supplies and the vehicles to do so. These officers used the example of the campaign of 1952. At Na San, on the Black River north of Hanoi, the Viet Minh had attacked a French outpost. When the French poured in additional troops, they beat back the Viet Minh, who were too weak to win the battle. Some members of Navarre's staff also emphasized that the Viet Minh lacked the artillery needed to defeat the French at Dien Bien Phu. French artillery was far superior, they said, and

French gunners could hit targets that the Viet Minh soldiers were too unskilled to hit. Finally, they said, any French army at Dien Bien Phu could be supplied by air from bases around Hanoi.

In July 1953, Navarre went to Paris to discuss the situation with the leaders of the French government. By this time, the French had decided that they could not win the war in Vietnam. They wanted to negotiate a peace agreement with Ho Chi Minh. Nevertheless, they were not ready to announce this policy. It would look as if the French had been defeated in Vietnam. Therefore, when Navarre talked about defending Laos, the government did not give him any firm directions. Navarre returned to Vietnam, having decided that he would look at French policy over the next year. As Navarre later put it, "Suppose that I had abandoned Laos on my own initiative and opened to the Vietminh the road to total victory: I would be branded today as the man who betrayed the honor of his country."

In October 1953, General Giap and his troops advanced toward Laos to begin a new invasion. Navarre had drawn up a plan called Operation Castor to deal with this precise situation if it arose. On November 20, 1953, French paratroopers descended on Dien Bien Phu. Assisted by their air force, which bombed the area, the French easily defeated the Viet Minh defenders and took control of the stronghold. Navarre then began to strengthen Dien Bien Phu with more troops. He also selected a successful tank commander, Colonel Christian de La Croix de Castries, to command the position.

Although Navarre was satisfied with his decision to retake Dien Bien Phu and put Castries in charge, there were still members of his staff who feared disaster. Colonel Jean Nicot, the commander of the French air force, warned that Dien Bien Phu was too far from Hanoi. Transport planes could hold just enough fuel to fly there, unload

Brigadier General Christian de Castries came from a long line of French military officers. Known to be a colorful character, Castries became the commander who would lead French efforts to counter Viet Minh attacks.

supplies, and return. If Dien Bien Phu were covered with fog or threatened by Viet Minh antiaircraft guns, the French planes might not have enough fuel to land and return to their bases. French fighter planes faced a similar problem. Unless they carried extra fuel tanks (which would limit their ability to maneuver), they did not have enough fuel to do much bombing and strafing before they would have to return to Hanoi. Nicot feared that the French position might be too exposed and too difficult to defend. Navarre was unconvinced, however, and he began to build up his position at Dien Bien Phu.

Meanwhile, General Giap's intelligence network kept him informed of French operations. Giap realized that the French might be giving him an opportunity to win an enormous victory. The Viet Minh had been defeated at Na San because they did not have enough troops and supplies to overrun the French position. Giap did not intend to repeat this mistake at Dien Bien Phu. Therefore, he

Colonel Christian de Castries

Members of Christian de Castries's family had served France for centuries. They had held high positions in the French government, commanded French fleets, and directed French armies in Europe. Castries himself had spent his entire career in the army. He was a champion horseback rider and a daring fighter pilot. He was a friend of Navarre's and had served as one of his subordinates. Navarre knew that Castries was a man of tremendous courage, who had been wounded in battle during both World War II and the Vietnam conflict and honored for his bravery under fire. Castries had also been highly praised by General de Lattre, who "held him in high regard, impressed by not only his courage and ability, but by his dashing style." He wore a jaunty red cap on his head and a red scarf around his neck. Castries was considered a playboy. There was even a rumor that three of the French artillery positions at Dien Bien Phu were named after three of his girlfriends. Navarre believed that Castries was just the right man to defend Dien Bien Phu. If the Viet Minh attacked the position, they would probably advance through the low hills near the base and try to overrun the stronghold. With the broad plain at Dien Bien Phu, French tanks would have plenty of room to maneuver and beat back such an attack. Castries would be just the commander to lead these counterattacks.

decided to concentrate a large force of 30,000 to 40,000 troops against the French stronghold. These included battle-hardened infantry divisions—the 308th, 312th, and the 316th. He also moved in the 351st heavy division. This group included an antiaircraft regiment, artillery regiments, and rocket units. The artillery would weaken the French positions. Then, the infantry would advance, blow up the French barbed-wire defenses or other fortified positions. Finally, the infantry would charge in waves to overcome the enemy. As the Viet Minh began their march toward Dien Bien Phu, Giap told them:

> The enemy is occupying a region of our beloved North-West. . . . We must repair roads, overcome difficulties and hardships, fight valiantly, endure hunger and cold, go up hill and down dale, cover long distances and carry heavy loads to find the enemy in his refuge to destroy him and liberate our compatriots.

Supporting the soldiers was a vast supply system that Giap had developed over the years of fighting. Thousands of porters carried food and ammunition for the army. The Viet Minh had also received transport vehicles from Communist China. These were used to carry heavier weapons. For these vehicles to reach Dien Bien Phu, however, the Viet Minh had to build many miles of roads through the jungles. These roads were carved out by volunteers, both men and women, who were committed to driving the French out of Vietnam. As they worked, the French regularly bombed the jungles from their aircraft. As the planes approached, the Vietnamese workers would dive for cover. Then, after the planes had left, they would resume their work.

To oppose the Viet Minh who were marching toward Dien Bien Phu, the French assembled a force of about 12,000 soldiers. Many of them were members of the French Foreign

Legion. Founded in the nineteenth century, the Legion was made up entirely of volunteers. They served in various parts of the French empire, such as Morocco and Algeria in North Africa, defending French holdings against attacks. The Legionnaires were tough fighters who believed they could defeat any Viet Minh army. In addition to the Legionnaires, the French had soldiers from their North African colonies, as well as sympathetic Vietnamese troops. Supporting the infantry were ten tanks as well as artillery that included howitzers and mortars. These were guns that could fire high arching shots into the hills to drive out the Viet Minh. If the Communists attacked, the French planned to fire at them with their heavy guns. As the Viet Minh advanced, they would hit barbed wire and minefields. These would slow them down, and they would then be hit by heavy machine-gun fire that would drive them back.

The French ran into problems in fortifying Dien Bien Phu, however. There was very little wood or concrete there to build strong fortifications to protect artillery or infantry. The soldiers were forced to build trenches instead. These offered only partial protection for men and heavy guns, especially since the French could not dig their trenches very deep because of poor soil. Nevertheless, the French were convinced that they still held a strong position. The Viet Minh, they reasoned, would place their artillery on the other side of the hills around Dien Bien Phu. These were the only places available to keep them safe from French artillery fire. The Viet Minh would have to fire over the hills if they wanted to hit French positions in the valley. The French believed the Communists lacked the ability to carry out such precision shooting.

As another part of the preparations, the French fortified outlying positions in the hills north, east, and west of their main camp. These positions were manned by French infantry to provide protection for the airfield and the main

French force. The Viet Minh would have to get past these positions before they could attack the main camp at Dien Bien Phu. By the time the battles for the outlying positions were over, the French believed that the Viet Minh would already have been driven away and would lack the manpower to continue their siege.

As the French waited, the Viet Minh approached Dien Bien Phu. Historian Jules Roy described the advance:

> Covering twenty miles by day, or fifty by night, the Vietminh divisions were advancing rapidly . . . marching along the sides of the roads. . . . each soldier carried his weapon . . . a bag, a thirty-pound bundle of rice slung over one shoulder, his individual shovel, water bottle and a little salt in a bamboo tube. He marched from dawn to sunset, or vice versa, with ten minutes' rest every hour. On arrival [at a stopping point] he dug trenches in which to take shelter and sleep. . . .

As the Viet Minh reached the hills surrounding Dien Bien Phu, they did not stop. Under the cover of the dense forests, the soldiers kept advancing. The Viet Minh did not plan to put their guns on the far side of the hills. They intended to set them up on the near side, facing the French position. They began to dig trenches on the hills facing the French in the valley. Their work was camouflaged by the trees and could not be seen by French planes. Often, the Viet Minh hid their guns during the day. Then, at night, the guns were brought over the tops of the hills and put into position. As the Viet Minh worked, they repeated these words:

> The ravines are deep,
> But none of them deeper than our hatred.
> Let us pull the gun behind us
> And the battlefield will become the graveyard of our enemies.

On February 3, 1954, the Viet Minh fired a few of their guns at the main French position. These guns were hidden under camouflage so the French could not seem them. Under the command of Colonel Charles Piroth, the French artillery fired back. Piroth thought he had successfully knocked out the Viet Minh gun positions. He was mistaken.

The Communists had built fake guns to mislead the French as to the positions of the real ones. Viet Minh troops set off explosives near these fake weapons to make it sound like guns were being fired. The French fired more than 1,600 shells at the false positions. French planes dropped bombs on them and French tanks fired at them. Piroth was unaware that he had hit only the fake guns. He still believed he could destroy the Viet Minh artillery. As he told Colonel de Castries, who was worried about the operation, "We shall at least see it when it opens fire. And then I'll smash it."

Unfortunately for the French, they had completely underestimated the ability of the Viet Minh to fight and win a major battle. General Giap had trained his soldiers to be an army of battle-hardened veterans. They also felt strongly about their cause, since they were fighting for the independence of their country. This spurred them to do what seemed almost impossible. Men and women built roads up the sides of steep mountains to transport guns up and down. Thousands of porters brought in enough food to feed the large army for days and weeks if necessary. The Vietnamese were also convinced that "they were taking part in a momentous event, an event which had penetrated to their very bones, giving them the conviction that they were going to win and that what had so far been much blind effort was about to culminate in dazzling light."

By contrast, the outnumbered French soldiers were professionals who had been flown in from other parts of the empire. They had no direct stake in fighting for Vietnam.

Indeed, the French political leaders had already come to the conclusion that the empire in Indochina might have to be abandoned. In addition, the French were defending a weak position at Dien Bien Phu. It was surrounded by hills that had been occupied by the enemy. The French artillery was exposed to fire. The only way to keep open the main camp was to supply it from the air. The French would now find out if that would be sufficient to bring them a victory.

In early March, General Giap had ordered Communist guerrillas to attack French planes at the airfields around Hanoi. The Viet Minh successfully damaged many supply transport planes that were intended to support the French at Dien Bien Phu. Giap had also launched diversionary attacks at other places in Vietnam. These attacks forced General Navarre to send his own troops and planes to stop the Viet Minh. In addition, he sent out planes to support these forces. As a result, he had fewer planes and soldiers to reinforce Dien Bien Phu. On March 10, General Giap issued a statement to his troops:

> Remember that it will be an honor to have taken part in this historic battle. Determined to destroy the adversary, keep in mind the motto: "Always attack, always advance." Master fear and pain, overcome obstacles, unite your efforts, fight to the very end. . . . The hour of glory has come.

At 5:00 P.M. on March 13, the Viet Minh launched their first major attacks on Dien Bien Phu. The artillery began to assault French positions during the last hours of daylight. The fortifications in the northern outposts, which were called Beatrice and Gabrielle, were hit first. At Beatrice, Viet Minh shells destroyed the French operations center, killing the commanding officers. Then, the Communist 312th division attacked under cover of darkness, and

Although the Viet Minh ultimately had the advantage at the siege of Dien Bien Phu, the French did have some successes. In a few engagements, the French not only pushed back the Viet Minh, but were able to capture enemy troops, such as this young Vietnamese soldier.

eventually overran the French position. The next day, the French launched a counterattack against the Viet Minh holding Beatrice, but they were beaten back before they could dislodge the Communist troops. General Giap realized how important it was for his troops to win the initial battle. This would boost their morale and toughen them to carry out a long siege.

After their victory at Beatrice, the Viet Minh attacked Gabrielle. The French sent reinforcements to hold off a Viet Minh attack by the 308th division, which began at 5:00 P.M. on March 14. The assault began with a bombardment from the Communist artillery designed to kill as many French soldiers as possible. Then, the Viet Minh infantry began its attack. For several hours, the French held back the Viet Minh assaults. Then, during the early morning hours of March 15, enemy artillery destroyed the French command position, knocking it out of action. The French launched a counterattack led by Colonel Pierre Langlais. He sent tanks and infantry, which included French and Vietnamese troops, against the Viet Minh positions. Meanwhile, the Viet Minh were also hit by fire from a French plane. As the French troops advanced, the Vietnamese troops of the French army found the enemy too powerful for them. The counterattack failed, and the Viet Minh held on to Gabrielle. At the same time, a third strongpoint in the north, called Anne Marie, was evacuated. With the other two positions lost, it could not be held against the Viet Minh.

Not only had General Giap captured the French northern outposts, but his artillery had also done severe damage to the French landing field in the valley. Planes were destroyed, huge holes were created on the runway by artillery shells, and the control tower was knocked out of action. Suddenly, the landing area that was supposed to enable the French to bring in continual supplies had become useless. Colonel Piroth realized that he had been completely unable to stop the Viet Minh artillery. Historian Jules Roy explained, "he took the grenade he carried in his belt, pulled the pin with his teeth and held it close to his heart." It exploded, killing him.

Once the Viet Minh had overrun the northern outposts, the fierce fighting stopped. Giap's troops did not stop advancing, though. Over the next ten days, they dug trenches closer and closer to the French outposts—called Dominique and Eliane—on the eastern side of Dien Ben Phu. In the meantime, the French officers at Dien Bien Phu saw that Colonel Castries could not successfully defend their position. The success of the Communists had been such a shock to Castries that he had lost his ability to make command decisions. Although Castries remained in overall command, day-to-day operations were taken over by Colonel Langlais and Lieutenant Colonel Marcel Bigeard. To supply their troops at Dien Bien Phu, the French began to drop in supplies by parachute. This was not effective at all. Some of the supplies did not land in the correct positions, so they did not reach the soldiers. To make matters worse, when the French went out to pick up the supplies, they were fired on by the Viet Minh. French planes also could not fly very low because Communist antiaircraft fire threatened to shoot them down. This made the parachute drops even more inaccurate.

As the end of March approached, General Giap's siege began to tighten around the defenders of Dien Bien Phu. The Viet Minh had used a combination of powerful artillery and fierce infantry attacks to take key French positions. In bloody hand-to-hand combat, they had been able to hold on to these positions in the face of heavy French counterattacks. There seemed to be little chance now for the French to escape defeat at the hands of the Viet Minh.

Victory at
Dien Bien Phu

French paratroopers were brought in to help defend Dien Bien Phu during the siege. Seen here marching along a mountain pass in the region, these troops were considered some of the best fighters in the French army.

On Tuesday night, March 30, 1954, a sound like rolling thunder broke over the heads of the French soldiers at Dien Bien Phu. The summer monsoon rains had begun. Already, they were filling the trenches with water and turning them to mud. The French had actually hoped the heavy rains might save them by forcing the Viet Minh to call off their attack. The sound that the French defenders heard was not thunder, however. It was the artillery of the Viet Minh. General Giap and his troops had unleashed a terrible bombardment against the French positions on the hills of Dominique and Eliane.

Dominique and Eliane lay to the east of the main French encampment and across the Nam Yum River. These hills were critical to the defense of Dien Bien Phu. If the Communists took control of them, they could fire down on the main French encampment from almost point-blank range. The French would then have no choice but to surrender.

Colonel Langlais had reinforced the strongholds of Dominique and Eliane. He had sent in more troops to defend these key areas so they would not fall to the Viet Minh. Sent to hold the positions was a combination of Moroccan, Algerian, and Vietnamese troops and French paratroopers. The paratroopers were considered the finest soldiers the French had in Vietnam.

The Communist bombardment was immediately followed by an overpowering assault by the Viet Minh infantry. Advancing from their trenches near Dominique and Eliane, the Viet Minh charged up the hills even under fire from the French machine guns. Although casualties were heavy, there were simply too many Viet Minh troops for the French to knock down. The Viet Minh outnumbered the French defenders by about ten to one. Within three hours, the French position had been completely overrun. Two key positions, called Dominique One and Dominique Two, had fallen to the Viet Minh. According to one observer, the Algerians who had been defending the position on Dominique Two were "running headlong down the hill toward the river." Fortunately for the French, they were able to retain control of a third position, Dominique Three, which prevented the defenders on Eliane from being outflanked.

Meanwhile, the defenders at Eliane were being pounded by the human waves of Viet Minh infantry. A position that the French called Eliane One fell to the Viet Minh. The Viet Minh also succeeded in capturing a section of Eliane Two. The French decided to launch an immediate counterattack to regain these important posts. With the help of their tanks, the French cut down many Viet Minh

infantrymen. They then drove the Viet Minh back from
Eliane Two and continued to hold the hill. Dominique Two
and Eliane One, however, were still controlled by the
enemy. The French launched another attack and regained
Dominique Two. The Viet Minh began to advance against
Eliane Two, but the French were able to drive them back.
The losses were very heavy on both sides.

As the battles raged over Eliane and Dominique, the Viet
Minh struck another French position. Called Huguette, it
was of a series of hill positions located just to the west of the
main French encampment. These hills guarded the airfield
at Dien Bien Phu. On the evening of March 31, the Viet
Minh attacked a position called Huguette Seven. At first,
they seemed to be successful in gaining control of the area.
Then the French counterattacked, and with the help of
mortars, grenades, and machine guns, drove the Viet Minh
off the hill.

The next day, Colonel Langlais received reinforcements. The men parachuted in from transport planes. The
additional soldiers were needed desperately, but bringing
them in was a big risk. All air operations were now very
dangerous, since the French controlled such a small area
around Dien Bien Phu. French planes were constantly
attacked by Viet Minh antiaircraft fire. The paratroopers
could easily have been shot out of the sky. There was also
no safe place for them to land. They were "dropped all over
the fortified camp, regardless of barbed wire, gun positions,
and radio aerials."

On the night of April 1, the Viet Minh renewed the
attack. A powerful assault led by the 312th division
struck Huguette. The positions at Huguette Six and
Huguette Seven were now under enormous pressure
from the Viet Minh, who were trying to take control of
the French airfield. In a bloody battle, the Communists
briefly gained control of Huguette Seven, only to be

pushed back by French tanks and infantry reinforcements. Colonel Langlais had won a temporary victory. Even so, he knew the French could not hold Huguette Seven for long, because the Viet Minh controlled the nearby hills and could quickly blast their way in once again. Langlais could not afford to risk any more troops at Huguette Seven, so he retreated from this position on April 2.

The monsoon rains had made reinforcing the camp at Dien Bien Phu very difficult for the French. On April 2, however, the weather did clear up long enough for more paratroopers to be dropped in. Although the new troops were more than welcome, the number of reinforcements was very small. It had become impossible to land large numbers of troops with General Giap's Viet Minh soldiers in control of the hills around Dien Bien Phu.

Over the next few days, the Viet Minh continued to assault the French positions on Huguette and Eliane Two. Each time, the waves of Communist attackers were beaten back each time by the French infantry and artillery. The Viet Minh had 800 soldiers killed, while the French lost 200. Their casualties may have been greater, but the Viet Minh could make up these losses. The French could not, since so few troops could land at Dien Bien Phu.

At this point, the French and the Viet Minh were battling not only each other but also the monsoon rains. The storms had grown even stronger, making life in the trenches even more unpleasant than usual. The monsoons kept the French from bringing in more reinforcements. At the same time, their heavy equipment was being depleted in the continuing battles. By April 6, the French had only four tanks available to send out against the Viet Minh.

General Giap's troops were also feeling the strain of a long battle that had not yet produced victory. As Giap put it:

As the Viet Minh bombarded the French defenses at Dien Bien Phu, the besieged troops were desperate for reinforcements. In an attempt to help the French forces, these paratroopers were dropped at Dien Bien Phu in March 1954.

Our offensive on the eastern hills of the central sector has obtained important successes, but . . . failed to reach all the assigned objectives. . . . We have therefore decided to continue to . . . tighten further our stranglehold so as to completely intercept reinforcements and supplies . . . utilizing trenches which have been driven forward until they touch the enemy lines, the tactic of gnawing away at the enemy piecemeal.

The French, however, had decided that they could not simply sit in their current positions and wait to be overrun. Major Marcel Bigeard decided that Eliane One must be retaken. The French began their assault in the early morning hours of April 10. The Viet Minh put up a furious defense, but the French moved in a contingent of flamethrowers that shot fire into the ranks of the Viet Minh and drove them out of their positions.

The battle was not over, however. Giap ordered elements of the 316th division to retake Eliane One. The struggle swayed back and forth, and forced the French to call in reinforcements. These new arrivals included soldiers from the Foreign Legion, French paratroopers, and Vietnamese. As the reinforcements approached Eliane One under the withering fire of the Viet Minh, the Vietnamese began to sing the French national anthem, the *Marseillaise*. The newly arrived French forces slammed into the Viet Minh and drove them from Eliane One, which remained in French hands. On the night of April 12, though, the Viet Minh struck again. They threw against Eliane One seven times more soldiers than the French had defending it. Still, the French would not give way. They held their position.

By the end of the struggle, the French were exhausted, but the Viet Minh losses had been staggering. As mid-April approached, General Giap had lost—killed or wounded—almost 20,000 troops, nearly 40 percent of his army. Viet Minh medics were having a difficult time treating the wounded. As historian Jules Roy put it,

> Six assistant doctors could not manage to give first aid to [hundreds of] wounded who were evacuated by convoys of porters toward the hospitals in the rear, after wounds had been dressed and broken limbs put in plaster. The most serious problem was the countless swarms of yellow flies which laid their eggs in all the wounds, which were teeming with maggots.

After facing such a huge loss, some commanders would have retreated. Giap, however, did not want a repeat of Na San. Ho Chi Minh had already signaled his willingness to make a peace agreement with the French. Before the peace negotiations began, however, the Viet Minh wanted an impressive victory. This would strengthen their position at the bargaining table. As a result, Giap decided to call in reinforcements from Laos to build up his army again and continued the siege of Dien Bien Phu.

In the meantime, the French were making a desperate appeal to their powerful ally, the United States, to help relieve Dien Bien Phu. By 1954, the U.S. government had already spent an estimated $2.5 billion to assist the French war effort. The United States viewed Indochina as one in a long line of dominoes. If it fell, other parts of Southeast Asia might also fall to the Communists. Therefore, U.S. President Dwight Eisenhower and his advisors wanted the French to remain in Indochina. Although the United States was willing to send aid, Eisenhower was not prepared to commit American troops to Indochina.

When the French effort to get the United States to conduct a massive air strike failed, General Navarre began to plan his own relief operation for Dien Bien Phu. This project was developed during April. By the time Navarre had started to gather the troops and supplies the operation required, however, the situation at Dien Bien Phu had grown much worse.

The French realized from intercepted Viet Minh radio communications that the enemy was bringing in more troops. These were supposed to make up for the heavy Communist losses at Dien Bien Phu. Eventually, Viet Minh forces reached 35,000, while the French had fewer than 5,000 men. This was less than half the original French force of 12,000.

The Viet Minh were continuing to build trench lines

closer and closer to French positions on Huguette. Their artillery scored direct hits on the French supply area, destroying a large amount of food stores that had been parachuted into Dien Bien Phu to feed the troops. In addition, Viet Minh antiaircraft guns—some of which had been supplied by the Chinese—were taking a heavy toll on French aircraft. Almost 50 planes were seriously mauled in April by the Communist gunners, who also downed eight French aircraft. By April 18, it had become clear to Colonel Langlais that he could no longer defend the French

Operation Vulture

For a brief period in early 1954, the U.S. government considered using air power against the Viet Minh at Dien Bien Phu. The operation, named Vulture, called for heavy U.S. air strikes. These would be launched from U.S. aircraft carriers in the Gulf of Tonkin. Such an overpowering strike, the French believed, might drive off the Viet Minh and rescue Dien Bien Phu. Some high officials in the Eisenhower administration supported the operation. Congress would not allow such an attack, however, unless the United States had the backing of its allies, such as Great Britain. Congress also wanted the French to begin an effort to give Indochina independence. The Eisenhower administration could not win support for Operation Vulture from its allies. The British, for example, strongly opposed any involvement. They feared that an air war would inevitably lead to the use of ground troops in Vietnam. They were also concerned that the Chinese might enter the war in support of the Viet Minh. U.S. Secretary of State John Foster Dulles, however, continued to pursue Vulture. At one point, according to historians, he even considered dropping atomic bombs on the Viet Minh army. It was Eisenhower who eventually put an end to any American military commitment. As he later wrote: "if the United States were, unilaterally, to permit its forces to be drawn into conflict in Indochina and in a succession of Asian wars, the end result would be to drain off our resources and to weaken our overall defensive position."

To protect themselves from Viet Minh fire, the French built traditional trenches, despite the poor soil that made these defenses less stable. Here, two French soldiers are running toward their trenches to escape an artillery barrage.

position at Huguette Six, at the end of the airfield. He ordered a retreat. Even during the evacuation, many French soldiers fell to enemy gunfire.

General Giap now turned his full attention to capturing Huguette One, which guarded one side of the French airfield as well as the main encampment. The position had already been heavily pounded by the Viet Minh. Supplies were short, and there were too few troops for the French to hold the stronghold against a determined Viet Minh attack. When that assault finally came, the French were forced to retreat, leaving Huguette One to the enemy. So much of Dien Bien Phu was now under Viet Minh control that the French effort to drop reinforcements was almost useless. The reinforcements would be killed as soon as they landed. Langlais and Bigeard decided to launch a counterattack with the few men they still had available and to retake Huguette One. The Viet Minh were too strong for the French attackers, however. Huguette One remained under Communist control.

The French were now running out of men, food, and ammunition. Their only hope seemed to be the monsoon. If it rained and blew hard enough, the Viet Minh might have to call off the siege. Dien Bien Phu might be saved. There was just a slim chance that this would happen, though. Giap believed that the monsoon was on his side. As he put it: "The French will soon be unable to hold out any longer under the monsoon. When they are forced to leave their flooded trenches . . . , victory will be ours." He was right. The rains made the trenches almost intolerable, and the monsoons made air drops of troops and supplies nearly impossible.

On May 1, 1954, General Giap began the final assault that he hoped would bring him victory at Dien Bien Phu. The Viet Minh attacked what was left of the French positions on Dominique and Eliane. Dominique Three was overrun, and Eliane One fell in the early morning hours of May 2. The Viet Minh continued to assault the French on Eliane Two. It was only a matter of time before this position, too, would have to be abandoned. The monsoon rains grew worse, and with them, the misery of the French defenders.

Over the next few days, Eliane Two fell to the Viet Minh. It was retaken by the French, only to fall again on May 7. The Viet Minh had tunneled under the position and ignited a mine that blew a huge crater in the position. Although some fighting continued, the Viet Minh had won a costly victory. The number of deaths on both sides was appalling. Viet Minh bodies were piled one on top of the other.

That same day, General Giap's forces overran the main French encampment. The French troops, who had held out for so long, began to surrender. White flags appeared over various French positions.

By 5:30 P.M., the Viet Minh had taken control of French headquarters. The French commander, de Castries, along with Colonel Langlais and Major Bigeard, surrendered. One final position, Isabelle, which lay to the south of Dien Bien Phu, fell to the Communists the next day. The siege was over.

After the fall of Dien Bien Phu, the United States became the main supporter of non-Communist Vietnam. Efforts by the Communist forces of North Vietnam to take over South Vietnam led to a lengthy conflict. Here, a machine gunner tries to protect South Vietnamese troops from North Vietnamese attack as they march.

The Impact of Dien Bien Phu

Why had the Viet Minh won the siege of Dien Bien Phu and the French lost? One of the primary reasons was that the French leaders had underestimated General Giap and his soldiers. General Navarre was convinced that the enemy did not have the capability to mount a long siege. Navarre looked at his experience in other Vietnamese encounters. The Viet Minh usually fought short battles. They would hit the French, and if victory did not come quickly, they would call off the battle. Navarre expected that the same pattern would be repeated at Dien Bien Phu.

Sieges are often won or lost because of supplies. If the army laying siege to an enemy can cut off supplies to the force under siege, then they can win a victory. Navarre did not think the Viet Minh

General Giap, the brilliant leader who defeated the French at Dien Bien Phu, is seen here reviewing his North Vietnamese troops.

would be able to cut off his supplies. With the airfield at Dien Bien Phu, he imagined that the French could successfully bring in a constant supply of food, weapons, ammunition, and troops. He did not count on the resourcefulness of the Viet Minh. First, they occupied the hills around Dien Bien Phu, where the French had never believed they would take a chance, since they seemed to be easy targets for the French. General Giap not only managed to put his guns there but to keep them hidden so the French could not hit them. In addition, the Viet Minh had been given Chinese antiaircraft guns to prevent French planes from landing at Dien Bien Phu. From their positions on the hillsides, the Viet Minh guns could easily shoot down any approaching French planes.

Navarre also underestimated the effectiveness of the Viet Minh artillerymen. He believed that his French gunners were far superior. Therefore, they would be able to knock out the Viet Minh guns before they could do any real damage to French planes or to the main encampment at Dien Bien Phu. Navarre was mistaken. The French were overpowered by the Viet Minh artillery, which cut off French supplies. The French could not land planes at Dien Bien Phu under the Viet Minh guns, nor could they parachute in enough supplies and men to make up for their losses. By the end of the siege, the French had very little food, almost no ammunition, and too few soldiers to withstand the final Viet Minh attack.

Whereas the French had difficulty maintaining their supply lines, the Viet Minh received a steady stream of supplies. With Chinese trucks and Vietnamese porters, General Giap's army fed itself and received all the guns and ammunition it needed to defeat the French. Before Dien Bien Phu, the Viet Minh had never kept an army in the field to fight a single battle for so long. Here, the Communists proved that they could do it. They also showed a willingness to sustain huge numbers of casualties to win a final victory.

After the fall of Dien Bien Phu, the French feared that General Giap might move his forces out of Dien Bien Phu and advance southward to threaten Hanoi. Hanoi was only one of the areas that General Navarre was forced to defend. One of his major problems was that he had to protect such a large territory with too few soldiers to do the job. Although Giap could strike wherever he wanted, Navarre was constantly on the defensive. The French had hoped to train local Vietnamese troops to help them defend the country. These soldiers often proved unable or unwilling to fight effectively. As a result, the French had to carry an enormous burden, which proved too much for them.

While the battle was still raging in Vietnam, a peace conference was being arranged to decide the future of Indochina. The conference included representatives of France, Great Britain, the Democratic Republic of Vietnam

(DRV, or the Communists), the Soviet Union, China, and the United States. The DRV was represented by Pham Van Dong, who called for the independence of Vietnam, Laos, and Cambodia. The French had no intention of giving in to the Communist demands. They were prepared to give up the area around Hanoi, because they feared an overwhelming Viet Minh attack, but they were not willing to leave Indochina entirely.

The Chinese, on the other hand, did not want the war to continue. Since late in 1950, they had been involved in a war against the United States in Korea. Earlier that year, Communist North Korea had invaded South Korea. The United Nations, led by U.S. forces, intervened to rescue the South Koreans. As the North Koreans were being pushed back, China stepped in on the side of North Korea. The Korean War continued for three more years, until it was ended by a truce in 1953. By the time of the siege of Dien Bien Phu, the Chinese government of Mao Zedong wanted peace and improved relations with the United States. Prime Minister Zhou Enlai, who headed the Chinese delegation at the peace conference, pressured the DRV to accept a compromise. Zhou flew from Geneva, Switzerland, to south China, where he met with Ho Chi Minh. The two men agreed on the immediate future of Vietnam.

A peace treaty was signed at Geneva on July 21, 1954. According to the treaty, Vietnam was split at the seventeenth parallel of latitude. Ho Chi Minh's Communist government would control the north. In the south, a non-Communist government would be led by Bao Dai. He appointed Ngo Dinh Diem as his prime minister. As part of the agreement, the Vietnamese would hold national elections within two years, aimed at bringing the country together once again under a single government.

Diem had no intention of permitting elections throughout Vietnam. He was too afraid that the Communists, who

Ngo Dinh Diem

Ngo Dinh Diem was born in 1901 at Hue, in central Vietnam. His father was a mandarin who served in the imperial government. Diem was raised as a devout Catholic and considered becoming a priest. He changed his mind, however, and attended the School of Law and Administration, where he was educated to become a French civil servant. Later, he was named governor of one of the Vietnam provinces in Indochina. He so impressed the French that, in 1933, he joined the government of Bao Dai as one of the emperor's chief ministers. Diem wanted the Vietnamese to have more power in the government, though. He soon clashed with the French and resigned. During the 1940s, when the Japanese controlled Vietnam, Diem pleaded with them to grant the country its independence. They refused. Although the Japanese were opposed by the Communists, Diem would not support the Viet Minh. He regarded them as ruthless criminals who would ruin Vietnam. At the end of the war, he was imprisoned by the Viet Minh. Soon afterward, he met Ho Chi Minh. Diem later recalled their conversation:

Diem: What do you want of me?

Ho: I want of you what you have always wanted of me—your coop-eration in gaining independence. We seek the same thing. We should work together.

Diem: You are a criminal who has burned and destroyed the country, and you have held me prisoner. . . . You speak a language with-out conscience. I work for the good of the nation, but I cannot be influenced by pressure. I am a free man.

Ho set him free. Later, Diem traveled to the United States. There, he became friendly with a number of American political leaders, including Senator John F. Kennedy. He urged the Americans to support a free and independent Vietnam. In 1953, he left the United States and met with Bao Dai. On June 18, 1954, he became the new prime minister of South Vietnam.

were popular in many parts of the country, might win. The United States agreed with him. The government of President Eisenhower was not willing to risk a Communist takeover of Vietnam. Eisenhower feared that it might lead to Communist control of Laos and Cambodia. So Diem sent his soldiers into the countryside to root out any Viet Minh who still remained in the south. By 1956, according to historian Stanley Kanow, "Diem had smashed 90 percent of the former Vietminh cells in the Mekong delta, and those that survived retreated into remote swamps."

Meanwhile, the regime of Ho Chi Minh was struggling in the north. Cut off from the rich rice fields of the Mekong Delta, the Communist government faced a severe food crisis. Ho was forced to import rice from China to feed his people. In addition, the Communists tried to impose land reform on the Vietnamese. They persecuted a number of peasants who owned relatively large parcels of land. Others were accused of working for the French. Thousands were tried and executed. The executions led to a revolt among the North Vietnamese, which was brutally put down by the Communists.

While the Communists were preoccupied, Diem had a golden opportunity to end their influence in the south. His own government proved to be just as unpopular as that of the North Vietnamese, however. Diem enriched his relatives and friends at the expense of the peasants of South Vietnam. The prime minister's close associates received lucrative business deals. Diem supported large landowners and refused to break up their estates to give the peasants more land. He also failed to provide more schools or better health care for the Vietnamese. As a result, Diem rapidly lost the support of the majority of the people.

In the countryside, the Communist guerrillas began to gain supporters. The Communists would appear in villages during the day, and even worked side by side with the peasants in the fields. Then, the Communists would drift

After Dien Bien Phu and the French withdrawal from Vietnam, the nation was divided. Ngo Dinh Diem was appointed prime minister of South Vietnam—the non-Communist sector. Despite his often corrupt regime, he was at first supported by the United States.

away when a government military force tried to capture them. Although Diem's soldiers could control a village for a short period, the Vietnamese peasants had no loyalty to the government. The political leaders lived far away in Saigon and never came out into the country. When the soldiers left, the Communists would return. Meanwhile, the U.S. commitment to the Diem government was increasing. By 1960, the Eisenhower administration had already funneled $1 billion in foreign aid to South Vietnam. Some of this money found its way into the pockets of officials in the Diem government, which was notorious for its corruption. Nevertheless, the Americans seemed to have no choice but to support Diem, since there was no other official who could replace him. Diem could not stop the terrorism in the countryside, however. The Communists were becoming more and more powerful. Government officials sent into the country to control the area were being murdered. In 1961, 4,000 of these officials were killed.

The following year, Diem decided to begin a "strategic hamlet" program. He proposed to force peasants into fortified towns so they could not help the Communist guerrillas. The efforts of the Diem government were supported by American helicopters with machine gunners. Even with the additional firepower, though, the Communists could not be driven away. By 1963, the government of President John F. Kennedy had committed 16,000 American military advisors to Vietnam. They were expected to assist Diem in his battle against the Communists. Nevertheless, the Communists continued to gain strength.

In 1963, Vietnamese generals, believing Diem could no longer lead the country, overthrew him. The generals were supported by the American government. Diem was later executed. A few months later, President Kennedy was assassinated in Dallas, Texas. He was succeeded by Lyndon Johnson. As president, Johnson increased American commitment to Vietnam. Johnson was convinced that the loss of Vietnam would also lead to a Communist takeover in all of Southeast Asia.

Over the next few years, American support of South Vietnam increased. By 1967, more than 400,000 U.S. troops were stationed in the country. President Johnson reasoned that such a huge force backed by American military technology could defeat the Communists. The French had believed exactly the same thing. The American adversary, however, was the same man who had defeated the French: General Giap. From the Communist base in North Vietnam,

Giap was sending 20,000 soldiers a month into South Vietnam. The communists had built a series of supply routes, known as the Ho Chi Minh Trail, to reinforce the guerrilla movement in South Vietnam. As he had done at Dien Bien Phu, Giap provided his soldiers with a steady stream of supplies to fight against the Americans.

Finally, in 1968, General Giap believed that he was ready to launch a major attack. The Communists targeted the large cities of South Vietnam, including Hue and Saigon. At the end of January, the attacks began. They were called the Tet Offensive, because they were launched during the Vietnamese lunar new year, known as Tet. The offensive caught the American high command by surprise. Like the French before them, they thought that the Communists were incapable of coordinating such a major assault.

Eventually, Giap's troops were beaten back, and the cities of South Vietnam were rescued. Still, the U.S. government realized that the North Vietnamese forces were too strong to be beaten. Tet had been an American victory and Dien Bien Phu had been a French defeat, but both battles had had the same outcome. The Communists had convinced their adversaries that they could not win a war in Vietnam. The American government opened negotiations with the North Vietnamese government. Over the next few years, U.S. forces gradually withdrew from South Vietnam.

By 1973, all American forces had left the country. Two years later, South Vietnam fell to the North Vietnamese. Although Ho Chi Minh had died several years earlier, Vietnam was once more united under one government. The Westerners had been driven out, and the country was finally independent.

200 B.C.   Chinese invade Vietnam.

100 B.C.   Chinese conquest of Vietnam.

A.D. 938   Vietnam becomes independent.

1431   Emperor Le Loi beats back Chinese invasion.

1535   Portuguese establish base in Vietnam.

1802   Gia Long becomes emperor of Vietnam.

1859   French capture Saigon.

1873   French capture Hanoi.

1887   France establishes empire in Indochina.

1890   Birth of Ho Chi Minh.

1907   Phan Boi Chau leads revolt against French.

938
Vietnam becomes
independent of China

1535
Portuguese establish
base in Vietnam

850

1550

Timeline

1917   Ho moves to Paris.

1919   Ho submits proposal to Paris Peace Conference calling for Vietnamese freedoms.

1930   Ho Chi Minh establishes Vietnamese Communist Party

1941   Japan takes over Vietnam.

1945   Japan defeated in World War II; Ho Chi Minh declares Vietnam independent.

1947   French regain control of Vietnam; civil war rages between French and Communists.

1952   Communist Viet Minh army occupies Dien Bien Phu.

1953   French retake Dien Bien Phu.

1954   Siege of Dien Bien Phu begins in March; Dien Bien Phu falls in May; Geneva Convention divides Vietnam into North Vietnam and South Vietnam; Ngo Dinh Diem becomes prime minister of South Vietnam.

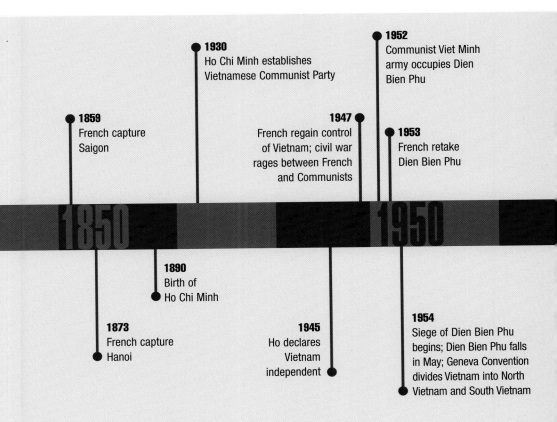

CHRONOLOGY

1956	Diem smashes most of Communist power in South Vietnam.
1963	Diem is overthrown and executed; United States sends 16,000 advisors to South Vietnam.
1967	United States has 400,000 troops in South Vietnam.
1968	Tet offensive marks turning point of Vietnam War; U.S. government opens negotiations with North Vietnam; American troops begin to withdraw from Vietnam.
1973	All American troops leave South Vietnam.
1975	South Vietnam falls to Communists; Vietnam is reunited.

CHAPTER 2, A LAND CALLED VIETNAM

Page 17: "The roof is very lofty . . ." Henry Yule, ed., *The Book of Ser Marco Polo* (New York: Charles Scribner's Sons, 1929), vol. 1, pp. 364–365.

Page 17: "this ancient land . . ." Stanley Karnow, *Vietnam: A History* (New York: Viking Press, 1983), p. 101.

Page 18: "Henceforth our country . . ." Ibid., p. 104.

Page 22: "the perverse religion . . ." Ibid., p. 67.

CHAPTER 3, CONQUEST BY FRANCE

Page 30: "[Using local peasants] . . . , he had . . ." Edward Doyle and Samuel Lipsman, *The Vietnam Experience: Setting The Stage* (Boston: Boston Publishing Company, 1981), p. 107.

Page 32: "Doumer built a refinery . . ." Ibid., p. 125.

CHAPTER 4, NGUYEN SINH CUNG (HO CHI MINH)

Page 38: "I have orders . . ." Edward Doyle and Samuel Lipsman, *The Vietnam Experience: Setting The Stage* (Boston: Boston Publishing Company, 1981), p. 116.

Page 39: "Nguyen the Patriot" Ibid., p. 120.

Page 42: "In all the French colonies . . ." Stanley Karnow, *Vietnam: A History* (New York: Viking Press, 1983), pp. 116–117.

Page 42: "was the most popular . . ." William J. Duiker, *Ho Chi Minh: A Life* (New York: Hyperion, 2000), p. 37.

Page 47: "Hour after hour . . ." Ibid., p. 59.

Page 48: "The decisive hour . . ." Ibid., p. 100.

CHAPTER 5, THE ROAD TO DIEN BIEN PHU

Page 51: "We hold the truth . . ." William J. Duiker, *Ho Chi Minh: A Life* (New York: Hyperion, 2000), pp. 109,110.

Page 53: "The airborne assault . . ." Ibid., p. 130.

Page 56: "The French air force . . ." Ibid., p. 197.

CHAPTER 6, THE SIEGE BEGINS

Page 61: "big administrative center . . ." William J. Duiker, *Ho Chi Minh: A Life* (New York: Hyperion, 2000), p. 251.

Page 63: "Suppose that I had . . ." Ibid., p. 306.

Page 65: "held him in high regard . . ." Stanley Karnow, *Vietnam: A History* (New York: Viking Press, 1983), p. 135.

Page 66: "The enemy is occupying . . ." Phillip B. Davidson, *Vietnam at War* (Novato, CA: Presidio, 1988), p. 49.

Page 68: "Covering twenty miles . . ." Ibid., p. 111.

Page 68: "The ravines are deep . . ." Ibid., p.113.

Page 69: "We shall at least . . ." Karnow, p. 170.

Page 69: "they were taking part . . ." Jules Roy, *The Battle of Dienbienphu* (New York: Carroll and Graf, 2002), p. 37.

Page 70: "Remember that it will be . . ." Davidson, p. 185.

Page 72: "he took the grenade . . ." Roy, p. 175.

CHAPTER 7, VICTORY AT DIEN BIEN PHU

Page 76: "running headlong down . . ." Jules Roy, *The Battle of Dienbienphu* (New York: Carroll and Graf, 2002), p. 204.

Page 77: "dropped all over . . ." Bernard Fall, *The Siege of Dien Bien Phu* (New York: Da Capo Press, 1985), p. 211.

Pages 79: "Our offensive on the eastern . . ." Ibid., p. 225.

Pages 80: "Six assistant doctors . . ." Roy, p. 226.

Page 82: "if the United States . . ." Fall, p. 312.

Page 84: "The French will soon . . ." Roy, p. 256.

CHAPTER 8, THE IMPACT OF DIEN BIEN PHU

Page 91: "Diem: What do you . . ." Karnow, pp. 216–217.

Page 92: "Diem had smashed . . ." Ibid., p. 227.

Davidson, Phillip. *Vietnam at War.* Novato, CA: Presidio, 1988.

Doyle, Edward, and Samuel Lipsman. *The Vietnam Experience: Setting the Stage.* Boston: Boston Publishing Company, 1981.

Duiker, William. *Ho Chi Minh: A Life.* New York: Hyperion, 2000.

Fall, Bernard. *The Siege of Dien Bien Phu.* New York: Da Capo Press, 1985.

Karnow, Stanley. *Vietnam: A History.* New York: Viking Press, 1983.

Roy, Jules. *The Battle of Dienbienphu.* New York: Carroll & Graf, 2000.

Worth, Richard. *Tet Offensive.* Philadelphia: Chelsea House, 2002.

Young, Marilyn. *The Vietnam Wars, 1945–1990.* New York: HarperCollins, 1991.

RICHARD WORTH has thirty years experience as a writer, trainer, and video producer. He has written more than 25 books, including *The Four Levers of Corporate Change*, a best-selling business book. Many of his books are for young adults on topics that include family living, foreign affairs, biography, history, and the criminal justice system.

TIM MCNEESE is an Associate Professor of History at York College in Nebraska. Professor McNeese earned an Associate of Arts degree from York College, a Bachelor of Arts degree in history and political science from Harding University, and a Master of Arts degree in history from Southwest Missouri State Univeristy. He is currently in his 27th year of teaching.

Professor McNeese's writing career has earned him a citation in the "Something About the Author" reference work. He is the author of more than fifty books and educational materials on everything from Egyptian pyramids to American Indians. He is married to Beverly McNeese, who teaches English at York College.